"Wise and wonderfully [...] of a book is like sitting down with a good friend who happens to know all the best-kept secrets of landing a job."
—*Michele Patrick,*
Award-winning Speechwriter

Your
BEST
Job Interview

Donna A. Bacon, Ph.D.

Your Best Job Interview

YourBestJobInterview@gmail.com

Copy Editor: Catherine Ard
Designer: Chet Kozlowski

Published in the United States of America

ISBN: 978-0-578-42006-6 (book)
ISBN: 978-0-578-42007-3 (ebook)

For Mom and Dad
I love you forever.

ACKNOWLEDGMENTS

Thank you to each and every colleague, job candidate, and client with whom I've worked over many years. It has been a privilege. Your experiences have taught me so much about the job interview process.

Dedicated and gracious readers have pored over and edited several versions of the book. I am indebted to them for their time, patience, diligent work, and steadfast support. A very special thank you to Christine Gallagher, Pina Rahill, and Elizabeth Vrato. Your contributions have been invaluable, and your spontaneity when I needed it most has been priceless.

My message would not have been delivered as clearly or effectively without the exceptional talent of my copy editor, Catherine Ard. Her diligence and precision have made all the difference. My deepest gratitude for your constant dedication, and your boundless energy and time. Thank you for challenging and teaching me.

The book would not be what it is without the counsel and guidance of Chet Kozlowski. His expertise impacted the content and organization of the book and ensured that the reader would stay personally invested. A heartfelt thank you for your unwavering support and confidence in me.

Thank you to my family for your love, and for respecting the time and effort it took me to write this book. Sadly, our parents did not see the completion of this project.

Contents

Why I Wrote *Your Best Job Interview*   xiii

PART I
Get the Basics Down   **1**

Chapter 1
Your Best Resume   **3**
   Your Resume Must Distinguish You   3
   Hard Skills vs. Soft Skills   4
   Fit Your Talent on One Page   5
   Soft Skills: Copy + Paste = Delete   10
   Career Objective (or Not)   11
   Strike Your Lists   13
   Oh My Gosh…the Hobbies   15
   Omit References   17
   Spill-check!   18
   Ready for Send Out?   18
   You Will Be Googled   19
   Don't Wait for Anything   20

Chapter 2
So, You're a Rocket Scientist. How Are   **22**
Your Communication Skills?
   Communication Is Key   22
   Verbal Communication   23
   Tame Your Verbal Quirks   24

Chapter 3
Interpersonal Skills Have the Last Word   27
    Meet, Greet, Treat—Repeat   27
    You've Got Personality!   29
    Managers Have Interpersonal Skills, Too   32

Chapter 4
What You Wear and How You Wear It   34
    What Are You Going to Wear?   34
    Business Formal or Business Casual?   35
    Grooming and Body Art   37
    Video Chatting: The Same Rules Apply   39

PART II
Crush the Interview!   41

Chapter 5
The Phone Interview Is the Hardest Interview   43
You Will Ever Have
    What Is an Interview Anyway?   43
    What You Have to Say and How You Say It   44
    Challenges of Being Invisible   45
    Benefits to Being Invisible   46
    Getting Situated   47
    Do Not Let Your Technology Hurt You!   48
    Say It with "Sparkle Tone"   50

Chapter 6
Interview On Site Every Chance You Get   52
    Why Is It So Important?   52
    You Need Practice   53
    Stay in the Game...of Power!   56
    Networking   59

Chapter 7

Why Should I Hire You for This Job?   **60**

The Question in Disguise   60

Tell Me About Yourself   61

Why Do You Want This Job?   62

What Are Your Career Goals?   65

What Are Your Weaknesses?   68

The Book Question   70

Chapter 8

Honesty Is the Only Policy (Positively!)   **73**

Always Be Honest and Positive   73

Explaining Poor Grades   74

Saying "I Don't Know"   75

Termination of Employment   77

Chapter 9

Why Have You Moved Around So Much?   **80**

You Will Be Asked!   80

Reasons for Voluntary Job Movement   81

The Job-hopper   84

A Layoff Is No Longer a Stigma   86

Chapter 10

What to Do About Timing   **87**

Timing Is Everything!   87

Manage Your Interview Scheduling   88

Manage Your Response to a Job Offer   89

Your Due Diligence   91

PART III
Take Nothing for Granted   **95**

Chapter 11
Having a Successful Interview   **97**
Does Not Mean Getting the Job
    What Defines Success?   97
    Answer the Unasked Questions   98
    You May Never Know Why You Were Declined   100

Chapter 12
Lunch Is Never Lunch   **104**
    Remember You Are on a Job Interview!   104
    Don't Let Your Guard Down   105
    It's Time to Eat   106

Chapter 13
It's More Than Just a Thank-You Note   **108**
    To Write or Not to Write…
        That is the Question   108
    One More Test to Pass   109
    Always Say "Thank You"   111

Chapter 14
Select the Right References   **112**
    Who Are Your References?   112
    Your Selection Criteria   113
    Coach Your References!   115

PART IV
Let's Talk Money   **119**

Chapter 15
Your Salary Requirement   **121**
   How the Talk Goes   121
   What Is My Salary Requirement?   122
   Quoting a Firm Number   125

Chapter 16
There Are Many Reasons to Take a Pay Cut   **127**
   There is More to Life Than Money   127
   Benefits and Perks   129
   Manage Your Ego   131

Chapter 17
Negotiate Professionally   **132**
   Do I Want This Job?   132
   A Game of Ping-pong   134
   Other Levers for Negotiation   136
   Don't Let Your Job Offer Be Rescinded 137

Chapter 18
Resign Your Job and Your Guilt   **142**
   Get Hired First!   142
   Some of Us Look Back   143
   The Counteroffer   144

Conclusion   **149**

Why I Wrote *Your Best Job Interview*

I have advised and coached job candidates for interviews for most of my career. I've heard countless anecdotes and addressed innumerable questions and concerns common to interviewees before, during, and after the interview process. I realized I was repeating myself, offering the same advice to candidates time and time again. Thus, I was inspired to write this book. *Your Best Job Interview* shares my observations, perceptions, preferences, and lessons learned related to the interview process. It readies you for your *best* job interview!

What qualifies me to advise you? I worked in corporate America as an analytics manager for an industry leader in telecom. I supervised teams; recruited, interviewed, and hired staff; and coached many employees through career development. I transitioned to executive recruiting, joining a premier firm in New York City. My expertise led me to clients who had analytical needs and candidates who were skilled in quantitative and technical disciplines. My scope broadened to include many indus-tries, and I mastered my ability to spot talent and place candidates into jobs that matched their interests and strengths.

The value of *Your Best Job Interview* is that it shares my unique perspective, shaped by experience in both indus-try and executive recruiting. I suggest new areas of focus and fresh ideas, emphasizing the not-so obvious aspects of the job interview process. Some perceptions are coun-terintuitive, stretching beyond the usual, brass-tacks ad-vice. The content is practical and useful; it is based on real interviewing experiences, including my own. The book has something to offer anyone who is prepping for any type of interview.

Typically, I coach candidates one-on-one, stressing what works on a job interview and what doesn't. This book does just that. It takes you through the job inter-view process in a way that's easy to follow. Or you can refer to specific topics in random order. Either way, I've packed each section with tips and wisdom from my years in the field. I will encourage you, boost your con-fidence, and help you maintain positivity, to take control of your own success. You may even come to enjoy your job market experience!

Thank you for reading *Your Best Job Interview*. You are the inspiration that led me to write this book. I hope our paths cross again.

—Donna A. Bacon

Part I

Get the Basics Down

CHAPTER 1

Your Best Resume

Your Resume Must Distinguish You

Does your resume make a positive first impression? Does it distinguish you? Does it have the power to get you an interview for the job?

In most cases, your resume is your initial contact with a hiring manager. It has the power to open or close a door for you immediately upon receipt.

The purpose of this chapter is not to teach you the mechanics of writing your resume, but rather to focus you on what your resume must *do* for you. *Your resume must distinguish you.* It must highlight your unique professional qualifications and separate you from the large pool of relevant talent that is your competition. Ultimately, it must get you an interview for the job. It must be *your best resume*.

Hard Skills vs. Soft Skills

Understanding the difference between hard skills and soft skills is key to writing your best resume.

Hard skills are your academic and professional credentials that can be proven by factual and typically documented evidence. For the most part, your resume is a presentation of your hard skills. These skills are the main determinant of a hiring manager's decision to interview you.

Your academic credentials include the schools or universities you attended, your earned degrees, honors, and awards. They also include scholarly works such as publications, patents, white papers, and presentations (that may be professional as well).

Your professional credentials are basically your work history. This includes the companies for which you worked, the jobs you held, and the time you spent in each role. This also includes exams, certifications, and licenses that are required of your job.

On the other hand, *your soft skills are your communication and interpersonal skills. These skills are less relevant for your resume, but they are critical for your interviews and hire.* You may provide examples of your soft skills on your resume, but you must *prove* them when you interview.

Fit Your Talent on One Page

Does it makes sense that a hirer could decide whether to interview you after reading only the first page of your resume? Of course it does. If there is nothing there worth exploring, why turn the page?

Address this challenge: write a one-page resume. Whether or not you use this resume for send out, it will force you to identify your distinctive marketable qualifications. Then work to present them in a comprehensive yet concise way. This exercise prepares you for your interviews. It puts your key qualifications and how to effectively discuss them in the forefront of your mind. And a one-page resume ensures that a hiring manager doesn't miss anything.

I recall reviewing a two-page resume that was written adequately but needed improvement. The candidate's

Ivy League education was buried on the second page. Unless you are so accomplished in your career that your Ivy League education would be assumed, it should be presented on the first page of your resume. This will ensure that a hiring manager turns the page!

In any case, *your academic and professional credentials should be quickly and easily identifiable on your resume.* A hirer will usually look first to see which schools you attended, what companies you worked for, and what jobs you held. Then for each role, he'll want to know about the work you did, how you applied your expertise, what business purpose it served, and what you accomplished. *He wants to know how you can contribute to the business.* If you are a fresh graduate with no employment experience, you would be presenting your academic projects in lieu of jobs. Present internships and volunteer work as well.

In constructing your resume, whether one page or not, use the standard bullet-point format to present your employment history in reverse chronological order. Limit your resume to a maximum of two pages (unless your unique experience warrants a longer resume).

Minimize the number of bullet points that describe each job. In some cases, stating the company name, your job title(s), and your dates of employment without any bullets is sufficient. For instance, a job you held that has no relevance to your current career path, one you held for a very short time (relative to your other jobs), or one you held so long ago that you barely remember it, needs no elaboration. You could omit these jobs from your resume altogether, as long as they don't create large gaps in your employment history.

Let's say your first real job out of school was as a bank teller, and after three years of service you were promoted to head teller and are now on a progressive career path in banking. While a student, you worked as a server at your local deli. Now that you have three years of professional work experience in banking, your employment as a server is irrelevant for your resume. It's admirable that you held a job while attending school, but your career-related experience now supersedes that. Including your job as a deli server on your resume would only distract from your focus on banking.

However, if you are a fresh graduate who has little or no career-related experience, any work experience you have is significant. For example, let's say you held two jobs in subsequent summers as a lifeguard and a library assistant. This work experience displays your willingness and ability to take initiative, assume responsibility, interface with customers, and provide leadership. It proves you are employable! This is very important when searching for your first professional job. As a fresh graduate, all of your real-world experience belongs on your resume.

If you are a seasoned professional who has had several different employers throughout your career, you will have a host of career-relevant jobs to include. Use your best judgment, although it's usually better to account for all the time you were employed versus having breaks in your resume. Breaks disrupt the presentation of your employment history and may call into question your career stability. A hiring manager has to get past your resume in order to interview you.

Be aware of the length of each job description. The number of bullet points that describe each job should be related to both the significance of the job to your career and the amount of time you spent in that job. Presumably, a job you held for five years should have a longer description than a job you held for one year, assuming both are career relevant.

Avoid redundancies! ~~Avoid redundancies~~! If you are promoted within a company and your job function remains unchanged, state all your job titles so your career progression is clear, but collapse the descriptions within the company so your bullet points are not repeated. I once read a resume that listed two adjacent jobs with exactly the same bullet-point descriptions. This was a good example of a bad resume. Not only was it poorly written, it touted stagnation. If this is true of your experience, you will likely have to address it on an interview. Why advertise it early on your resume?

Avoid repetition across companies as well. To the extent your roles are similar, your job descriptions will also tend to be similar. Write your resume so it captures as many of your *different* qualifications as possible. Repeating the same ones takes up space and adds no value.

Soft Skills: Copy + Paste = Delete

When addressing your soft skills in particular, keep this simple rule in mind: *if you can copy and paste your text to someone else's resume, delete it.*

"Excellent communication skills" is one of the most popular assertions of soft skills. It typically falls under the heading of "Highlights," yet ironically, it highlights nothing. These words can be copied and pasted to every applicant's resume. How does this make anyone stand out?

"Team player," "Hard working," "Goal oriented," and "Deadline driven" are other soft skills that are highlighted on many resumes. When these traits appear repeatedly on resumes under review for the same position, they do not help a hirer decide whom to interview. And imagine these descriptors on the resumes of a senior accountant, an accomplished writer, and a fresh graduate looking for her first job. These assertions fail to differentiate not only applicants who are competing for the same job, but also ones in a completely different industry and stage of career!

If you refer to your soft skills on your resume, describe them by example. You might note your interpersonal skills by referencing the customer-facing component of your job (e.g. sales, customer service) and sharing your above-average customer satisfaction ratings. Or you might spotlight your communication skills by indicating your lead role in key presentations to senior management. Examples, not assertions, support your qualifications for hire.

A former professor of mine was the one who taught me that soft skills should not be asserted on a resume. He explained that such empty assertions are nothing more than one's opinion of oneself. Instead, I must demonstrate my soft skills when I interview. Apparently he had read the same list of soft skills on too many students' resumes.

Career Objective (or Not)

Every job seeker has heard somewhere along the way to begin a resume by stating a career objective. This is a good idea for entry-level or junior candidates. A career objective lets a hiring manager know you've begun to think about your desired career path. It gives her an idea of the direction in which you're headed and the type of role you are targeting.

A career objective that is skills focused versus job focused gives you flexibility in your job search. Logistically, it enables you to use the same resume to apply to many jobs because it identifies the core skills you will bring to *any* job. More importantly, it may open doors for you. Managers usually know of more vacancies in their organization than the one to which you applied. By stating your desire to use your skill set, you create an opportunity to be considered for other openings that also require your skills.

For example, if you are targeting a role as an economic research analyst, you might state your career objective as seeking to use your skills in economic analysis, market research, financial analysis, data management, and forecasting. This may prompt the manager to consider you for other open positions that require your skills—not only the economic research analyst. Perhaps a data analyst, budget analyst, market researcher, or demand forecaster role is open. Any of these jobs could launch your career in economic research and analysis, and put you on the career path you want. And if it's a company you are eager to join, it gets you in the door!

Experienced candidates may forgo a career objective. If your resume is well written (i.e. your qualifications are clear), an objective is often redundant. And at some point, your career is well underway and your employment history speaks for itself. You may include a *career summary,* however, and if you do, make sure it adds value. High-level and vague intros (which often assert soft skills) can weaken the resume of an accomplished candidate. The details of your work are far more important to convince a hiring manager how you will contribute to the business.

Strike Your Lists

Lists on resumes are overrated. They provide a nice visual summary but are ineffective for differentiating individual talent when the competition is similarly skilled.

Job candidates within the same field generally know many of the same topics. Fresh graduates who study the same major tend to follow a similar curriculum. Senior-level professionals share many of the same high-level leadership abilities. Lists of skills, coursework, fields of

13

study, and areas of expertise all begin to read the same across comparable resumes. And as a list grows inordinately long, it becomes impossible to identify an applicant's relative strength in any area. It raises the question of whether the person has expertise in anything.

There are exceptions. In some fields, the absence of a list of skills would be a gross omission. For instance, if you are a computer programmer or software developer, a list of hardware, software, databases, platforms, and other applicable tools is expected on your resume. A hiring manager wants to know upfront in which environments you have knowledge and experience. This informs his decision to interview you.

Another exception is works of outstanding achievement. These include publications, patents, white papers, and presentations. If these works are required for the position you are pursuing, cite them in a list. The hirer will then know where to find them if he wants to review them in detail. If these credentials are not required for the job, or if there are too many to list, note them as "available upon request."

Oh My Gosh...the Hobbies

I am amazed by the hobbies I've seen listed on resumes: reading, dancing, cooking, fishing, meditating, playing with the kids, the Lakers, binge-watching TV shows... What? Wow.

I understand why job applicants put hobbies on their resumes. Hobbies offer a glimpse of a candidate's personal side. If your hobbies pique the interest of an interviewer, they may help break the ice. For applicants with little to no work experience, hobbies flesh out an otherwise skeletal resume. They tell an interviewer something more about you than where you went to school.

However, hobbies are irrelevant to your qualifications for hire. No one is hiring you because of your hobbies. (At least we hope not.) So if you can use the space on your resume more productively, exclude them. As your career progresses, hobbies begin to distract from the focus of your resume.

Extraordinary talents or outstanding achievements are different. They belong on your resume. For example, a piano virtuoso, a triathlete, a skilled artist, an Olympian, and a national champion of any kind all exhibit rare and impressive talents. Mensa members and Eagle Scouts have achieved superior honors and rank. World travel is also a significant feat. Unique talents and life experiences do more than reveal a candidate's personal interests. They offer insight into one's intellectual capacity, aptitude, physical and mental stamina, and character.

Likewise, volunteer experience that expresses your passion for the job or career you are pursuing belongs on your resume. For example, if you desire a career in nursing, your experience as an aide in a hospital augments your job qualifications. The same is true for volunteer positions that call for leadership and integrity, such as serving your local community or government.

Hobbies, on the other hand, are not distinctive accomplishments. Many people read, dance, and cook, and those who have small children generally find time to play with them. Hobbies may have some relevance in your interview process, however. "What do you do for fun?" is a common interview question, and it gives you the floor to discuss your ballroom dancing, favorite author, or trophy catch. (Choose your topics wisely and discuss moderately!) Don't worry that no hobbies on your resume gives the impression that you don't have any. If an interviewer is interested in your hobbies, he will ask you about them.

Omit References

Listing professional references on resumes has become quite common. However, *you should not put professional references on your resume—ever*. Your resume is a presentation of *your* professional, marketable qualifications. This is the information a hiring manager needs to know in order to decide whether to interview you.

Typically, you are not asked to share references with a prospective employer until you are close to an offer. You will have to provide them before you're hired, and the hirer expects to receive them at that time. When you are asked for references, expeditiously provide them— but not on your resume. Use all of the space on your resume for *you*.

Spill-check!

Sending a resume out the door with spelling mistakes is irreversible. Some resumes begin by highlighting "Exceptional attention to detail," then continue with spelling errors and typos. *At the very least, spell-check your resume!* Spelling errors and typos are just plain sloppy and can shut down your candidacy immediately.

I recall when a candidate did not advance to the interview stage because she misspelled the name of her employer on her resume. Some errors are inexcusable. I have even seen typos in candidates' phone numbers and email addresses. If a hiring manager cannot find you, how are you ever going to be hired?

Ready for Send Out?

Before you send your resume anywhere, read it carefully and have several people proofread and critique it. Your readers should have different appropriate backgrounds so you get feedback from varied perspectives. Ask them to copyedit as well as read it for content. Inquire if your resume distinguishes you. Does it separate you from your competition? Will it get you an interview for the job?

When you are confident it's your *best* resume, it is ready for send out. But there is one more critical step to complete before you release it.

You Will Be Googled

Manage your online presence *before* you send out your resume! Hiring managers often look beyond your resume to decide whether to interview you. Review your professional profiles that are sitting out in cyberspace, such as those on LinkedIn and your personal website. Make sure they are professional in appearance and content, and be sure to check your spelling. (If you do not have a LinkedIn profile, I encourage you to create one.)

Clean up your social media! Today potential employers have access to your personal information that you or someone else has made public. This includes Facebook photos, blogs, and anything else they find via an Internet search. Google yourself, and either remove or make private any questionable information you manage. *You don't want anyone doubting your good judgment.* It could be the difference between getting an interview or not.

Don't Wait for Anything

After you send out your resume, you'll naturally become anxious waiting for a response: Yes? No? Maybe? Don't wait for anything. When we wait, we become discouraged. This slows down our progress. Apply to a job that interests you, and then apply to another. Keep applying. *The key to a successful job search is to keep moving forward!*

Some companies move quickly, and others flow with glacial speed. You may hear back from a hiring company within days, weeks, or months, and often never at all. Imagine the deluge of resumes coming in to a firm that is hiring. There are likely hundreds of qualified applicants who are competing with you. And, where the company stands in its hiring process—whether it has started, stopped, or never started at all—is impossible to know.

Keep track of all the company contacts to whom you sent your resume. Reach out to them, and follow up. Did they receive your resume? Is the position still open? Are they interested in your candidacy? You should reach out within a few days of sending. Calling is proactive; it shows courage and confidence. Emailing is passive; your message may sit, and possibly get lost, in the recipient's inbox. Distinguish yourself—*call!* Whenever you don't reach a person live, always leave a voicemail and ask for a call back.

Even after you follow up, don't wait for anything. Keep moving forward. Maintain your momentum and energy, and stay proactively engaged until you land the job you want!

CHAPTER 2

So, You're a Rocket Scientist. How Are Your Communication Skills?

Communication Is Key

Time and time again I marvel at the exceptional credentials of candidates with whom I've spoken. It takes extraordinary brainpower to accomplish such outstanding achievements. But alas, regardless of how well educated or accomplished you are, you must be able to communicate.

Your best resume will get you in the door to interview for a job that interests you. But your personal and professional presentation of yourself will ultimately determine the outcome of your job interview.

Verbal Communication

Verbal communication refers to the ability to speak and understand the common language. Strong verbal communication skills are essential for any interview. You must understand the interviewer, and he must understand you, for a meaningful dialogue to take place.

Strong verbal communication is both efficient and effective. To be efficient, you must be articulate, clear, and concise. To be effective, you must be intelligent, comprehensible, and persuasive. To be both, your thoughts must be collected, organized, and focused. You should address only key points when speaking, being direct yet thorough in your delivery. Active listening is essential to stay on track with the discussion. You must comprehend the exchange, and your questions and responses must be on point.

Rambling is neither efficient nor effective. If you are long-winded, talk in circles, go off on tangents, and never get to the point—or get there after the listener has stopped listening—you will not progress to the next step in the process. And never interrupt an interviewer while she is speaking. Interrupting is rude, and it shows that you are not actively listening.

Strong verbal communication skills are important for *every* job, because in *any* job, you will have to verbally communicate with someone—your boss, advisor, colleague, coworker, subordinate, customer, or client. And excellent communication skills are necessary to be an effective leader in any business. Employers look for these skills when they are hiring.

So, you're a rocket scientist. How are your communication skills? Being a rocket scientist is very impressive, but being a rocket scientist with great communication skills is unstoppable!

Tame Your Verbal Quirks

There are many ways to improve your verbal communication. Simply practice! Talk with your friends. Take a public speaking class, or join a public speaking club. Attend professional talks; focus and listen. If the common language of an interview is not your native tongue, listen to language recordings and pay close attention to pronunciation and grammar. Speak the language as often as you can. Talk, and keep talking.

If you have any verbal tics (we all do), such as repeatedly saying "um," "uh," "you know," "again," "like," or "you know what I mean," practice taming them. These words are fillers between thoughts and serve no purpose other than to let us keep talking while we are thinking. Instead, slow down, take a silent moment to think, and be conscious of the words you are saying. For instance, "I would meet with my team. We would discuss next steps, deliverables, and deadlines," is a more intelligent delivery than "I would, like, meet with my team. We would discuss, like, you know…next steps, deliverables, and, um…deadlines. You know what I mean?"

Poor speaking habits detract from your qualifications, so you must manage them. Try recording yourself talking and answering practice interview questions off the top of your head. Listen to how you sound. If you hear obvious tics, work on eliminating them. If you speak too quickly, slow down. If you speak too loudly or too softly, adjust your volume accordingly. Think moderation! If you detect a nervous giggle or other quirks, work on refining them. Be mindful of your regional dialect. Correct use of grammar is important. *The goal is to sound intelligent, confident, and polished.* We all must, like, you know, learn how to communicate. You know what I mean?

CHAPTER 3

Interpersonal Skills Have the Last Word

Meet, Greet, Treat—Repeat

Interpersonal skills refer to the way one interacts with others—how one meets, greets, and treats another person or people. If your interpersonal skills are poor, chances are you will not get the job.

The meet and greet protocol in the American culture starts with a firm, friendly handshake. A handshake shows openness, confidence, trust, and respect. When you shake a person's hand, you should be standing. Look him in the eye and smile. This lets him know you're present, attentive, engaged, and happy to be meeting him. This sets the tone for the entire interview. A firm handshake also marks the end of a meeting.

You must demonstrate strong interpersonal skills when you interview because people hire people with whom they want to work. Likeability is key. We all want to enjoy our work day as much as possible. And, when we work long hours, we want to enjoy the company of our coworkers with whom we burn the midnight oil. Interviewees who are pleasant and friendly, and appear to have it all together, have a much easier sell than those who are unpleasant, moody, rigid, or rough around the edges. We seldom hear interviewers conclude, "I don't like this guy. Let's hire him!"

Strong interpersonal skills are required for every job because people must be able to work together effectively. They have to be able to share ideas and agree on action items, deliverables, and deadlines. They have to assign tasks, critique work, manage productivity, and resolve conflict. And they should be able to do so amicably, respectfully, and professionally. This is universally known as "team-work." No one looks to hire a high-maintenance, conflict-prone, "problem employee." No one wants to work with one, and certainly no one wants to manage one.

You may have excellent credentials and get the interview, but your *interpersonal skills have the last word.* Why? Because they have the power to secure a job offer or shut down your candidacy immediately. If the fit is not there, there is no forcing it. The interview may continue as scheduled, but the hirer's decision to pass has already been made.

You've Got Personality!

Be aware of your personality type when you interview. Your interpersonal skills reflect your personality, and the hiring team's perception of you determines whether they hire you. *While you are letting your personality shine, the interviewers are deciding whether they can —and want to —work with you.*

Regardless of your personality type, your interpersonal style should be pleasant, polite, friendly, and always professional when you interview. You must be someone the hiring team wants to hire!

Whether you are extroverted, introverted, high-strung, laid-back, even-keeled or something else, you have the potential to be the strongest contributor on the team. But you have to get through the interview process successfully for the hirer to know that.

If an interviewee appears uptight, she may be perceived as too nervous to handle the pressure of a high-stress workplace. Or the hiring team might be afraid she would knock their relaxed work group off-kilter. On the other hand, a laid-back candidate may be considered unenthused or lackluster about the job. A hiring manager might be concerned that he would drag his feet when facing critical deadlines. At the extreme, a "free spirit" might be perceived as completely unmanageable.

If a person is timid, he may appear to lack the confidence necessary to work on highly visible projects. And he may seem unlikely to handle tough clients effectively. On the other hand, a friendly and gregarious interviewee may appear very comfortable when interviewing, but sne needs to be aware of when to stop talking.

Energy level is very important. High energy often suggests high performance. Folks with high energy are attractive hires to a manager with a tremendous workload. He needs new hires who are charged up and eager to work. Someone with low energy may give him pause. Is this person really up to the demands of the job? Will he be productive? Energy also spreads. A smart manager looks for positive energy to increase the productivity of her team. Negative energy drags an organization down.

Embrace your personality, and be aware of it when you interview. You cannot control how others perceive you. You can only control how you present yourself. Don't hesitate to ask a trusted friend or colleague if there is anything about your personality that you might keep in check. You will make an indelible impression when you interview, so you want to know how your interpersonal skills may be perceived. Always ensure you are remembered as *professional!*

Managers Have Interpersonal Skills, Too

While an interviewer is observing your interpersonal skills, you should be observing his. You may find you're not the right fit for a particular organization, or better said, they're not the right fit for you.

When I was fresh out of graduate school, I interviewed with a handful of organizations at a professional job convention. One employer had the worst interpersonal skills I had ever seen. A sea of anxious job candidates were gathered in a hotel lobby, each waiting for his name to be called by an interviewer. When my name was called, the interviewer immediately turned around and headed to the interviewing room, leaving me trailing behind. When I caught up with him at the door, he walked into the room and somehow the door closed before me. I opened it (not sure why), walked in and sat down at the table where he was seated. He never offered me his hand to shake, and barely looked up from his list of questions to make eye contact. I knew immediately that this was not a manager with whom I wanted to work. I was also skeptical of an organization that would select this individual to represent them. I quickly scratched that organization off my list, and moved on.

In fact, at the same convention many years later, I was interviewing junior candidates for a job I had open on my analytics team. One young man sat down with me to be interviewed, and after a brief handshake and introduction, his phone rang. He answered the phone, stood up and walked a few feet from the table, and started talking to his friend. I was dumbfounded by his lack of courtesy and expectation that I had the time and interest to wait until his call was over. I'm not sure who ever hired this young man. It wasn't me.

CHAPTER 4

What You Wear and How You Wear It

What Are You Going to Wear?

When I was a manager in business, a woman on my team asked me if I would coach her in preparation for her in-person interview for a top MBA program. We conducted our informal coaching session over dinner, and I started by nonchalantly, though intentionally, tossing out the question, "What are you going to wear?" She fumbled a bit because she hadn't yet selected her interviewing outfit. Then she asked me, "What *should* I wear?" I said, "Wear *anything*...as long as you are better dressed than everyone else in the room!" We laughed, and she got my point immediately.

When you interview, you must look neat, clean, sharp, smart, and always professional. You are framing an impression for your interviewing audience, and as the saying goes, you only have one chance to make a first impression. The point is to be as well dressed or better dressed than your interviewers. This will assure your confidence.

Business Formal or Business Casual?

Years ago it would have been said that formal business attire is appropriate for every job interview. For men, formal business attire means a business suit, either black or navy blue, with a white long-sleeved collared shirt, understated necktie (solid red or blue are common), and black dress shoes. Similarly, for women, it is a black or navy blue business suit (skirt or slacks) with a white or soft colored blouse, and low-heeled, closed toe, black or navy dress shoes, respectively. All clothing must be neatly pressed.

Today there are many office environments that are business casual, and some are just plain casual. Startups, tech companies, and creative agencies are often known to boast casual dress, including jeans, shorts, T-shirts, and flip-flops. If you're advised by an interview coordinator to dress casually, then respectfully do so. But always look neat and smart. And don't let your casual attire lead to too-casual posture. This can compromise your professional appearance.

For the corporate world, even in a business casual environment, interview in a formal business suit. Formal business attire is simply most impressive. It reflects your respect for yourself as well as your appreciation for your audience. And formal business wear makes you feel professional. It affects how you sit, stand, and carry yourself. It increases your confidence, and your confidence affects your interview. Your attire also influences the way others relate to you. They will treat you professionally and respectfully, and take you seriously if you are smartly dressed.

Early in my career, I interviewed with a prestigious research institution and showed up wearing my brand new black business suit, toting a new burgundy leather briefcase. I thought this was appropriate dress for a job interview. The interviewing team was very comfortably dressed in loose fitting pants, untucked shirts, and sandals. At first, I felt like a total misfit, but tried not to let it shake my confidence. Actually, I sensed an air of appreciation from the team for having dressed formally to impress them. I got the job offer. This experience led me to believe you can never go wrong with a business suit.

If you have any doubt about what to wear to an interview, ask the interview coordinator. You want to look your best, but you also need to be in touch with your audience and the respective industry. Err on the side of formal business wear, and use your best judgment. You are more likely to be excused for wearing a suit to interview with a startup than for wearing flip-flops to interview with a bank.

Grooming and Body Art

A job candidate once asked me if it was okay to sport a goatee to an interview with a boutique consulting firm. He stopped by my office the day before his interview and asked if I thought he should shave. What a confident and self-aware individual! I couldn't say for sure whether a goatee would or would not matter in this case. But, why take the risk? The gentleman decided to play it safe and shave. He wanted to be completely confident about his personal appearance for the interview.

I would reason the same for body art—namely, tattooing and piercing—which has become very popular in recent years. I don't know whether body art would impress or offend an interviewing team, but if it's not visible, it can't be judged. If you know your interviewing audience would appreciate a display of your artistic style, then present yourself as freely as you deem appropriate. Just keep in mind that if any personal adornments distract the interviewers' attention from your qualifications, it could hurt you.

The goal is to present yourself professionally. Be keenly aware of your personal hygiene. Be conscious of your hair; long or short, it must be clean and neat. Your hands and nails must be impeccable. Avoid flashy nail polish. Minimize your jewelry. Forgo perfume, cologne, or after shave. If someone sneezes because of something you are wearing, it could be very embarrassing. Freshen your breath. *Don't give anyone a reason to prejudge you negatively.* If your audience is offended by you in any way, it could cost you the job.

Video Chatting: The Same Rules Apply

Today many interviews are conducted via video chatting applications such as Skype and FaceTime. Video chatting enhances a phone interview or is a precursor or substitute for an in-person interview. The same rationale regarding your dress code and grooming applies. The interviewer can see you, so your appearance must impress him. Whenever you interview in person or via video, you will be judged on *what you wear and how you wear it.*

Part II

Crush the Interview!

CHAPTER 5

The Phone Interview Is the Hardest Interview You Will Ever Have

What Is an Interview Anyway?

A job interview is an information gathering and sharing session. It's your opportunity to gather and share all the information you need to decide whether you are interested in a specific job. It's a company's opportunity to gather and share all the information they need to decide whether to hire you. *The company is interviewing you, and you are interviewing the company!* The more information you gather and share, the closer you come to finding a job that suits you.

The job interview process typically begins with a phone interview, and if it is successful, moves on to an in-person interview. If you are lucky, there will be only one of each type, and you will get a job offer! However, there may be several phone or on-site interviews within the process. This depends on the number of decision-makers needed to interview you.

Know this: a hiring company may stop the job interview process with you at any time. You must always be professional, and stay the course. Your goal is to get through the entire interview process successfully.

What You Have to Say and How You Say It

The phone interview is the hardest interview you will ever have. Why? Because you are judged solely on two criteria: 1) what you have to say, and 2) how you say it. If you do not pass the phone interview, the process ends for you.

Criterion #1, *what you have to say,* reflects your background and knowledge. You'll share your education, skills, and experience. These should all be presented on your resume and are, in fact, what got you invited for the phone interview in the first place. So, know your resume!

There is little, if any, room for you to manage the outcome of a phone interview based on what you have to say. You either have the qualifications for the job or you don't.

On the other hand, Criterion #2, *how you say it*, is manageable for you. It will *make* or *break* your interview.

Challenges of Being Invisible

A phone interview is challenging because the interviewer doesn't see you. You cannot impress him with your formal business attire, your professional demeanor, or your firm handshake. He can't see the sincerity in your eyes or the attentiveness with which you're engaged in the interview. *How you say what you have to say is all he has to go on.*

A greater challenge for you is that you don't see the interviewer. You cannot read any constructive feedback from his body language that might help you steer your interview. You can't see if he's distracted, raising his eyebrows, rolling his eyes, shaking or nodding his head, or falling asleep. You can't gauge whether your answers are too long or too short, on the mark, or way off base. You don't know whether he's fully engaged and interested or bored and multi-tasking because in his mind he has already dismissed your candidacy.

Benefits to Being Invisible

There are also real benefits to being invisible to an interviewer. Capitalize on this. Prepare a good old-fashioned cheat sheet to refer to during the call. This should be a list of bullet points noting your key attributes, including examples. The purpose of the sheet is to make sure nothing essential to your candidacy gets missed during the interview. Be sure to include a few intelligent, thoughtful, well-crafted questions to ask.

Phone interviews are relatively short in duration. The interviewer is trying to gather and assess a lot of critical information in a short period of time. You don't have much time to impress him, so be concise. If he needs additional detail or explanation, he'll ask a follow-up question or ask you to elaborate. You may also initiate providing further information if it's needed.

Getting Situated

Your convenience aside, it is best to conduct a phone interview from your home versus your office. Business ethics notwithstanding, it's a big mistake to have your boss or coworker walk in on you or overhear you while you are interviewing. If you have to take the call at work, find a private place where you know you won't be interrupted for the entire duration of the call.

When conducting a phone interview from home, situate yourself away from your computer, at either your desk or dining table to receive the call. Place a hard copy of your resume and cheat sheet in front of you so they are fully visible for quick and easy reference. You should be able to refer to both documents instantaneously and seamlessly throughout the interview. Sit up straight with your feet on the floor so you stay alert. Do not allow any distractions in the room whatsoever—no music, television, food, children, or pets.

I once phone-interviewed a gentleman whose dog was in the room with him. A parcel carrier approached the front door, and the dog went berserk. The man lost all concentration while trying to tame the barking dog, and I could barely hear what he was saying. It simply does not occur to us to remove a pet from our interviewing area (or to remove ourselves from our pet's domain). Try to anticipate possible distractions and prevent the ones you can control.

Do Not Let Your Technology Hurt You!

Today technology is our greatest virtue and our greatest vice. Since most of our telephone communication is done via cell, most of our phone interviewing is also done via cell. But cellular reception is often unreliable, sound crackles, and calls drop. Most interviewers are busy professionals who are taking time out of their overbooked workday to interview you. Don't expect them to be patient and understanding when it comes to poor sound quality or a dropped call. Do your best to secure a landline when you phone-interview. If there is not one available, place yourself where you *know* the cellular reception is good and reliable. *Do not let your technology jeopardize your interview!*

I recall when a candidate's call dropped on a first attempt to phone-interview with a reputable firm. The hiring manager was reasonable and scheduled a second attempt, advising the woman to use a landline. She disregarded his advice, and the call dropped a second time. At this point, the candidate's judgment was called into question. Managers look for sharp people who know how to use their time and their manager's time wisely. This interviewee failed the interview before it ever started.

Video chatting adds another dimension to the technological challenge, and it's steadily growing as a preferred alternative to phone interviewing. If you are invited to video chat, make sure you are comfortable with the application the interviewer will be using. Practice using the technology and rehearse before you interview. The benefit of video chatting is only realized when it's done properly.

Finally, before you interview, move all hand-held electronic devices out of your reach and turn them off. Do not let anything ring, chime, hum, buzz, chirp, beep, or vibrate during your interview. We all have a natural human addiction to technology, and this can hurt us. Do not text! No email. No Internet surfing. And no social media! The distraction will break your concentration and destroy your momentum. The hiccup in your communication will make it obvious you are otherwise technologically engaged. *Do yourself a favor. Unplug for the interview!*

I have phone-interviewed people who were in moving cars, on moving trains, and boarding aircraft. The convenience of technology is immeasurable, but the interviewer must be able to hear you. Unless the person who is interviewing you would himself interview while in motion, your judgment might be called into question. An interviewer expects you to treat an interview as the most important thing you are doing while you are doing it. How important could your interview be if you haven't even ensured the person can hear you?

Say It with "Sparkle Tone"

Now that the interviewer can hear what you have to say and how you say it, she is listening to hear if you really *want* the job. You may say all the right things, but to convince her that you're serious, you must say it with "sparkle tone"!

I remember prepping an outstanding candidate for a phone interview with the head of a small analytics firm. His credentials were extraordinary, so I wasn't concerned about what he would have to say. I told him, "If you want to land this job, let them hear that sparkle tone!" It was a spontaneous choice of words, but he got my point: when you interview, the tone of your voice must demonstrate your interest, enthusiasm, and passion for the job. *Assuring a hiring manager that you want the job is every bit as important as having the skills to do the job.* And it often makes the difference between getting the job or not.

CHAPTER 6

Interview On Site
Every Chance You Get

Why Is It So Important?

An on-site interview is an inside look at a company—the people, the work culture, the team dynamics, and the office environment. You really have to interview on site to begin to know what a job is, who the people are, and what the work environment is like. Some interviewees walk into companies feeling excited about a prospect, and leave not wanting the job. Others go in feeling lukewarm, and leave chomping at the bit to be hired.

Only after interviewing in person can you make the best assessment of whether an opportunity is right for you.

You Need Practice

Whether you are on the job market for the first time, have not interviewed for years, or are a seasoned veteran of job interviewing, you need practice. Then when you find the job of your dreams, you'll be ready to nail the interview. Experience is the best practice! To get experience, *interview on site every chance you get.*

Whenever you interview in person, you are on from the moment you show up at the front desk to the moment you are escorted out the door. Your knowledge, skills, experience, and aptitude are being evaluated. Your appearance, attitude, energy, confidence, and overall demeanor are being assessed. You are judged from the time the interview begins until the time it ends. All that said, you must try to calm your nerves! You have been invited to interview, so there is already something about you that appeals to the hirer. You are there to see if the opportunity appeals to you as well.

Be on time to the interview. In fact, arrive at least fifteen minutes early to refresh yourself before you begin. Punctuality demonstrates responsibility, respect, and interest. It is professional!

Bring a notebook (such as a business portfolio) so you can jot short notes to help you formulate questions for the interviewers. Take this opportunity to learn as much as possible about the job, the industry, and the people. They will say many things about their work and field that you'll want to remember and research later. Ask each interviewer for a business card so you have their contact information and can recall their names and roles after a whirlwind of interviews.

Throughout the entire interview, be flexible! Regardless of how your interview agenda reads, you may or may not meet the people listed there. Availabilities change. Some interviewers may be bumped from the agenda, and some added to it. Others may be tapped on the shoulder and asked to fill in on the fly. People are very busy, and things happen. Don't let an organization's disarray jeopardize your interview.

54

Some interviewers will have studied your resume, and they will be prepared for you. Others will be reading your resume for the first time. *Always interview as if the interviewer has not seen your resume.* This way you'll be sure to give a complete representation of your talents and skills without omission. If an interviewer has already studied your resume and wants to skip ahead, she will let you know.

Expect your skills to be tested during the interview. If you are a writer, expect to write. If you're a programmer, expect to code. If you are a marketing professional, be prepared to pitch your creative marketing plan to a phantom client. If you're a financial analyst, expect to crunch numbers.

Anticipate case studies, puzzles, and brainteasers that test intelligence, aptitude, problem-solving, and strategic and critical thinking. You won't be able to predict which case study or puzzle you'll encounter on an interview, but experience will help you better handle the element of surprise. The same is true for personality tests. You'll never know for certain what is expected of you. You can only hope you have enough personality to pass it!

A formal presentation may be required of you so the hiring team can observe your presentation skills. If you are given the freedom to select your topic, choose wisely so you can use the same presentation again for other interviews. This will optimize your interview prep time going forward and help you through Q&A sessions. Questions you've heard before should be easier to tackle. Any boost to your confidence improves your performance.

Many years ago, I was interviewed by a panel of five people for an analytical job with a major industry leader. Someone handed me a pencil and paper, and the team began firing questions at me. The chilling experience has stayed with me to this day. I needed practice! (I did manage to get the job offer. Lucky day, I guess.)

Stay in the Game…of Power!

One of the big mistakes job candidates make is to withdraw from an interview process before it's over. Of course, it makes sense to withdraw if you don't want the position under any circumstances. But when you quit early, you never know what you could be missing.

Some candidates exit an interview process because they are indifferent about the opportunity and feel badly about wasting the company's time. This is where many interviewees' understanding of the interview process breaks down. Choosing to interview is *not* a commitment to accept a job if it's offered. It makes sense that you would be indifferent about a job you know little about. Likewise, a company is not committing to hire you because you agreed to interview. You are one of a select (though potentially large) pool of applicants who the company has chosen to learn more about. So you are no more wasting the company's time than the company is wasting yours. Go explore the opportunity fully! You may be surprised to see that your interest level increases after you learn more.

Never end an interview process because you are counting on an alternative prospect to materialize. Your decision to opt out must be based solely on your opportunities that are certain—that is, your status quo and any other job offers already in your hands. You have no guarantee of any other outcome until the interview process is over.

Of course, if you get an offer for the job of your dreams, it makes sense to accept it and shut down all of your other interviewing activity. But if you have other prospects worth exploring, keep interviewing. You never know what an opportunity is until you get an offer.

A job offer gives you invaluable information about the job market. It tells you what your talent is worth in a specific market. If you secure several offers, you'll learn that some companies pay more, others less. Certain industries pay more, others less. Job offers also reflect the costs of living in respective job locations. All this information is necessary when evaluating and comparing opportunities.

A job offer also gives you bargaining power. It proves you are marketable! It gives you leverage in negotiating other job offers because it's proof that another firm is competing for you at a certain price. If you interview for multiple jobs, you will appreciate the bargaining power that a job offer gives you.

Foregone interviews are foregone job offers. So stay in the game. You don't want to have any regrets because you stopped an interview process too soon.

Networking

Interviewing is networking. Networking begins by meeting people. *Anyone you meet has the potential to help you.* If you are not hired this time, your network may help you find another great opportunity next time.

Networking is relationship building. Reach out periodically with a friendly email or phone call to professionals you've met. Introduce yourself to someone you would like to know. Ask a question, share an insight, suggest an event, or extend an invitation for lunch or coffee. Meet again, and get to know each other. The people with whom you build relationships become your references and endorsers. Stay in touch with them so they remember you!

Networking can open doors for you in countless ways. These doors may open today, tomorrow, or anytime in the future. *To be successful, you must create opportunity for yourself.* So go interview, and network every chance you get!

CHAPTER 7

Why Should I Hire You for This Job?

The Question in Disguise

When you interview, you may be asked many diverse questions. Some are high-level questions regarding your professional interests and career goals. Others are low-level ones addressing the details of your work experience. Some questions test your general aptitude for learning. Others test your ability to problem-solve or to think creatively, critically, or strategically. Some are behavioral in nature and others logistical, about your job search in general. Some are positioned formally, and others come up casually in conversation.

Know this: regardless of the question you are hearing, each and every question you are asked in a job interview is **"Why should I hire you for this job?"** *in disguise.* As you formulate each response, think about why you should be hired for the job. Each answer is an opportunity for you to prove it.

Tell Me About Yourself

Why is "Tell me about yourself" such a nerve-racking start to any interview? Theoretically, you know yourself. So you shouldn't have any trouble telling someone about yourself. Right? Wrong!

Telling a hiring manager about yourself is difficult because it prompts a story from you rather than a simple answer. You may not be sure where to begin or end your story, and the middle can also get muddled if you find yourself rambling with no end in sight.

Your talk should be professional, not personal. You should limit it to about one minute, and be practiced. Start by introducing yourself with a few words about your current employment or academic situation and why you are looking for a job. This will put you on track to talk about what really matters.

"Tell me about yourself" really means, "Tell me about yourself so I will hire you." What is it about you that makes you interested in the job? What is it about you that makes you qualified for it? What is it about you that makes a hirer want to hire you? Knowing what the hiring manager needs to be done and articulating how you are the one to do it is the way to tell her about yourself.

When a hiring manager says "Tell me about yourself", she should be getting an answer to the question: "Why should I hire you for this job?"

Why Do You Want This Job?

Every hiring team wants to hear that its prospective hires have a passion for its business—or at least a healthy appetite for learning and growing with it. Without exception, you will be asked, "Why are you interested in working here?" or "Why do you want this job?" A wrong answer can shut down your candidacy immediately. "I'm just seeing what's out there," and "I just need a job" are fatal responses. Companies do not hire people who are interviewing everywhere out of curiosity or desperation. *The right answer is a sensible and compelling reason why the role, the company, and the industry all appeal to you.* Interviewers want to hear that you are genuinely interested in their business or cause. They want to hire someone who *wants* the job, not someone who is ambivalent about it.

Do your homework. Research the company and industry before you interview. This gives you the context in which to understand the job. Job descriptions are a good start, but for similar roles, they tend to read the same across many companies and industries. Your research and interviews are what let you understand the job.

Know the company's products or services, its customers, and its competitors. Know its history, reputation, brand, and market share. Educate yourself on recent news, business development, product launches, and other public information. This includes corporate citizenship, philanthropy, and public service. Be ready to engage in a meaningful dialogue, to ask and to field relevant questions. Positioning yourself as an informed candidate is very important. *An interviewee who hasn't taken any initiative to learn*

something about the company and industry is not a serious con-
tender. Nor is one who has no questions.

Doesn't it make sense to ask about some unique challenge facing the company today? Don't you want to know
the company's strategic vision for the future? What about
the team's immediate needs and why they are hiring? Can
they give you an example of a project currently underway? If they hire you, what will you be working on when
you start? Don't you want to know what you might be
getting yourself into?

Perhaps you are interviewing with a Fortune 500
company because you'll be able to develop and grow
your long-term career internally with a global industry
leader. Maybe you're interested in joining an ad agency
because it will demand your creativity in an exciting and
dynamic environment where you know you will thrive.
You may want to join a technology startup for the high-
risk, high-reward entrepreneurial challenge. Perhaps an
opportunity in retailing or hospitality will enable you to
develop your customer-service skills in a familiar industry. Perhaps an R&D opportunity with a biotech company
will put you on a ground-breaking path of discovery. Or

advocating for the cause of a non-profit organization will fulfill a personal mission for you. Whatever the company and industry you are targeting, have thoughtful reasons why you want to work there and good ideas of how you will contribute to the business.

Know the people you will be meeting! Research them and know their backgrounds. What is their experience, tenure with the company, length of career, education, and field of specialization? LinkedIn is a good place to start to look for this information, but if the individuals are well experienced or specialists in their field, dig further. Read any papers, publications, or presentations you can find, so you are informed and can ask intelligent questions. Listen attentively so you can engage in dialogue. *Give each interviewer every reason to hire you.*

What Are Your Career Goals?

Anyone who has ever interviewed for a job has probably heard the question, "Where do you see yourself in five years?" or "What are your career goals?" This is a question some candidates dread. Many are focused on today, tomorrow, next month, or maybe next year. Few can see beyond that—let alone five years out.

Even though interviewees expect the career goals question, many have no idea how to answer it. This isn't because they have no goals. It's because many personal circumstances and external factors affect our decision-making, and these dynamics are ever changing. It is hard to sound confident and convincing answering a question when you truly do not know the answer.

Your long-term goals should be consistent with your motivation for interviewing for the job at hand. Why would a hiring manager hire you for a job that doesn't put you on a path to your career goals? She wants a new hire who is excited about *this* job and the direction in which it's headed. She wants you to stay, grow, and be successful. Share your career goals with the manager and convince her that the position for which you are interviewing will lead you there.

For example, if you are interviewing with a financial services firm, do not say your career goal is to join a leading digital company. This may be true, but it doesn't help your case for financial services. If you're not excited or passionate about finance, you will probably leave as soon as your golden digital opportunity comes along. If you are interviewing with a management consulting firm and disclose that your long-term goal (in the short term) is to lead a fintech startup that is already underway in your basement, why would the consulting firm hire you? Your devotion will be to your own "baby," and you probably won't make the full commitment that consulting requires. Instead, research the career path for the job you are pursuing, and make a strong case that it's the direction in which you're headed.

Experienced professionals generally have an easier time with the career goals question. Part of their career is behind them, so usually some of their goals are already realized. An individual on a steadily progressive career path might want to continue to grow her industry knowledge and skill set, and ultimately actualize her leadership potential. One with a more diverse or volatile career profile may be an expert who desires a challenging job that adds value to a business regardless of industry or level. As we advance in our careers and learn more about ourselves, our goals naturally become clearer.

What Are Your Weaknesses?

Oh, no...the weaknesses. Unless you've done a lot of interviewing, you are probably a little wary when you hear the question, "What are your weaknesses?" A weakness, by definition, is a negative, so the question prompts a negative response: "I can't do this," or "I don't know that." But there is no place for negatives in a job interview. So how do you reveal a weakness without being negative and hurting your chances of getting the job?

Think of a weakness as a developmental opportunity — some skill you would like to learn or improve. Employers look for people who possess the desire and initiative to take on great challenges and learn new things. A developmental opportunity turns a weakness positive, and thus, becomes a strength. You should position it that way. When you interview, focus on what you *know*, not what you don't know. There will always be something required of a job that you don't know, but what you know is that you can learn it!

Let's say that a job requires advanced Excel skills, but your skills with Excel are beginner level at best. Approach the discussion by sharing what experience you do have with the software and emphasize your desire to learn and to master it. If you have other strong skills that the role requires, your limited Excel skills may not be a deal breaker. You might mention that the required use of Excel is something that attracts you to the job. It offers you a new challenge and growth opportunity.

Another approach is to identify personal attributes that can be considered weaknesses but are also strengths. Perfectionism is a good example. Perfectionists strive for flawlessness. This may be a weakness in a role where time spent trying to be perfect is unproductive. However, it's a prerequisite for a job that requires precision. In any case, it is always a strength to be meticulous in your work, so admitting you are a perfectionist usually leans in your favor.

When you're asked about your weaknesses, do not disclose something unequivocally negative. Don't share that you occasionally forget to set your alarm and are sometimes late for work. A manager does not want to hire someone who demonstrates irresponsibility and laziness. Nor does he want to hire someone senseless enough to disclose this during an interview.

Finally, never respond by saying that you do not have any weaknesses. Of course you do. Think about those attributes you could improve to be more successful in your job. Ask someone who knows you well to have a constructive conversation with you on the topic. If you really think you do not have any weaknesses and say so, no one will want to work with you.

The Book Question

One of my own interviewing experiences made me realize that every question in a job interview really is, "Why should I hire you for this job?" Early in my career, a hiring manager asked me, "What was the last book you read, and why did you read it?" I was interviewing for a position as a revenue forecaster. My immediate thought was, "Where is this curve ball coming from, and where is it going?!" I thought the question was irrelevant to my interview entirely.

Why would a hirer ask me about the last book I read while I was interviewing for an analytical role? Was it to get a glimpse of my personal side—to know what type of books I read or whether I read at all? Was it to see how I would handle the element of surprise? Was it to test whether I could collect my thoughts and summarize material coherently and concisely on the spot?

Of course! *This curve ball was thrown to test many different aspects of my job candidacy.* I learned that regardless of why the book question (or any question) is asked, I must continually provide convincing evidence that the manager should hire me.

My first experience with the book question was a rough one. I had just finished reading a fascinating piece of historical fiction that depicts the life of a young adult who makes an extremely controversial life-defining decision. As I was summarizing the book aloud, I was thinking, "Why did I choose such a provocative story to recount during a job interview?" I think I did okay with the summary, but when the hiring manager asked why I had read the book, I missed a good opportunity. I naively said that the book was a gift from a friend, which was true but completely unimpressive. This response did not demonstrate any initiative on my part nor did it offer any interesting reason why I read the book. It added no positive value to my interview.

At the time, I thought the book question was a one-off. Then I got the same question a few weeks later in an interview with another company. This time I discussed a recent read that is a popular best seller used as a professional development tool in corporate America. The book was very easy to summarize because of its nature, and my motivation for reading it was to learn, grow, and improve myself professionally. What more could a hirer want to hear?

CHAPTER 8

Honesty Is the Only Policy (Positively!)

Always Be Honest and Positive

There will always be questions or topics of discussion in a job interview that push you outside your comfort zone. There are three examples below. Address such topics carefully, and always be honest. Never give an interviewer the impression that you are lying, hiding something, or trying too hard to defend yourself. *No employer ever hires a person he perceives as dishonest. Not ever.*

There will also be questions during your interview that prompt a definitive negative response. How you position the discussion is critical. Employers hire people with a positive attitude who want to learn and grow in their business. *No one makes a positive impression by being negative.* So when you have something negative to say, say it in a positive way. When you interview, **honesty is the only policy (positively!).**

Explaining Poor Grades

If you are a fresh graduate or junior-level job applicant, your grades are important when you interview. If you have a GPA less than 3.0, you may be asked about it. Be forthcoming and accountable. Don't be defensive, and never blame an instructor. As you acquire more work experience, your grades become less important.

It is easier to explain a poor grade in Latin versus Marketing if you are a business major or young marketing professional. You may have studied a foreign language as an elective to challenge yourself beyond the required business curriculum. Your knowledge of Latin is less relevant to your job search and probably doesn't matter at all. However, the fact that you studied such a difficult subject is impressive in and of itself, and this makes the discussion a positive one.

It's a bit harder to explain your poor grade in Latin if you are a foreign-language major. The proof is on your transcript, so address the question directly. If you failed a course or two, admit it, and do your best to explain why. Perhaps Latin was a requirement of the foreign-language program. You enjoyed the experience of learning it, but it challenged you more than you anticipated.

If strength in academics is most important to the hiring team and your academic record is lacking, you may not progress in the process. However, if your honesty and desire to tackle new challenges are really what matter, you may still be very much in the running.

Saying "I Don't Know"

When you are asked a question about something you do not know, you may reply "I don't know" or "No," but don't stop there. A definitive negative response closes a door that might otherwise lead to a positive discussion of what you *do* know. A lack of knowledge or experience is always a developmental opportunity. *If you are asked a question you cannot answer, answer a question you can!*

First of all, always know *something* about *everything* listed in a job ad for the role you are pursuing. The job description is an obvious hint of what might be asked of you on the interview. If there is some requirement disclosed there that you do not know, research it before you interview. You should at least acknowledge that you are familiar with the topic and be able to address it appropriately if you haven't yet had a chance to learn it.

Perhaps you are an analytics professional with experience in many different technical areas, and you are asked about tools that you have not yet used on the job: "What is your experience with big data tools?" Presumably you are keeping abreast of the latest technologies and have done some research in preparation for your interview. Address the question as best you can, but don't worry if you lack the specific experience the manager is looking for. Instead, answer the question: "Are you able to learn and master big data tools?" Discuss the tools and platforms you know, and provide examples of how your experience is transferable to the big data space. Use this opportunity to showcase your expertise and aptitude to learn new technologies quickly. Say if you are self-taught in any of these areas. This signals your ability to teach yourself the tools in question.

Perhaps you are applying for a job that requires fluency in Spanish, but you have little to no knowledge of the language. If you are fluent in any language besides your native tongue, say so. Your proven ability to learn foreign languages is a very competitive skill for this job. Or if you studied Spanish in school, discuss it. Maybe you are looking to master the language or grow your language skills further. Divulge that one of the major reasons you are interested in this job is because it requires you to learn Spanish and use it. The question you hear may be: "Are you fluent in Spanish?" Instead, answer the question: "Are you able to become fluent in Spanish?" Of course you are! Always keep the discussion positive.

Termination of Employment

One of the toughest topics you will ever address in a job interview is why you were fired. Regardless of the direction in which the discussion heads, *never defame another's name or character*. Explain the situation without complaining, whining, or blaming any other party. If you were terminated, there must have been some circumstances that involved you that did not align with your manager's expectations or the company's policies. When explaining the situation, try to offer a lesson learned from the experience that will enable you to prevent the same result in the future.

If your manager's judgment was that you underperformed on the job, perhaps your understanding of the demands of the job was different than what was expected of you. Maybe you didn't anticipate the evening or weekend work hours that were required. This led to work-life balance issues that were impossible to resolve given your family responsibilities. Ultimately, your production fell short of your manager's expectations, and you were let go. Or perhaps the skill level required for the job was beyond your knowledge, and the learning curve was steeper than either party expected. This was just not the right job for you. You learned you need to vet the job, the work hours, and the manager's expectations more thoroughly by asking more direct questions going forward.

Maybe you were terminated because there was inter-personal conflict across the team and you were told things weren't working out. Perhaps you observed after joining that there were personality conflicts within the group that undermined the team's performance. In your opinion, adding another person to the mix further exacerbated the problem. You were the newest employee aboard, so you were the one who was let go. You learned you must observe and focus more keenly on team interaction when you interview. You have to ask questions about the nature of work projects and the role each member plays to get a better read on the overall health of the organization. Be sure you do this while you interview!

On the other hand, if you were terminated because your behavior was in conflict with company policy, clearly say so. This may be a difficult discussion, but be honest, and own it. Share any important lessons learned, and present yourself as ready to move on productively to your next opportunity.

CHAPTER 9

Why Have You Moved Around So Much?

You Will Be Asked!

Almost without exception, job seekers are asked about their job movement. A hirer wants to know the reason why you left each job and moved to the next one. This is a fair question. He is interested in your career progression, but he also wants to make sure you are a steady employee. Don't overwhelm him with unnecessary details. Be honest and positive, and keep the discussion brief and relevant.

Reasons for Voluntary Job Movement

If you left a job for career advancement, your explanation is a simple one. You may have moved for a promotion, a management opportunity, or other professional development. Hirers look for people who demonstrate initiative and ambition in achieving their career goals. They also appreciate a sensible career path. If you changed jobs within the same industry, it's generally assumed that you aspire to grow and diversify your experience for a long-term career in that industry. On the other hand, if you changed industries when you moved, expect a follow-up question asking why. You may simply have found a great opportunity in a more stable or exciting industry, or a better fit where you could see yourself growing your career over the long term.

Maybe you left a job because you did not get along with your boss. There is no way to express any type of interpersonal conflict without putting doubt in the interviewer's mind that you are a problem. *Avoid discussing any interpersonal conflict during your interview.* Discuss other limitations of the role or environment instead. Perhaps you weren't challenged by the work or there wasn't enough of it to keep your work group busy. Maybe there was no ownership of projects so you did not feel empowered. There may have been obstacles to internal movement or career progression, and you didn't see a future there. For instance, continual headcount reduction or employee turnover could stagnate an organization indefinitely. All these reasons for job movement reflect positively on your candidacy. Hiring managers listen to hear that a candidate seeks challenge and career growth.

Another reason you may have left a job is because you weren't paid well enough. *Never mention your low salary as the reason you are looking for a new job. It raises the question of whether you are a poor performer.* If your current salary is below market, it suggests your prior merit increases reflected below-average work performance. You don't want to put any doubt in the hirer's mind about your potential value to the company. Managers hire above-average performers exclusively. Why would anyone hire a below-average performer? Talk about money in terms of opportunity. It is true that you are seeking a new job to increase your salary. That is, by definition, a better opportunity. There is no reason to mention money.

Maybe the job was just the wrong fit for you. Short stints are characteristic of this misfortune. Perhaps the position you were hired for was redefined between the time you interviewed and the time you started the job. This does happen! Or maybe your skills were underutilized, or the work did not align with your career goals. These are valid reasons to leave a job. Sometimes it makes good sense to cut your losses and move on.

Job movement may also be due to personal circumstances—some of which are more difficult to broach than others. For example, complicated family situations involving divorce, child custody, illness, and aging parents may be hard to discuss. If you need to delve into these areas so your explanation makes sense, be as brief and direct as possible.

Simpler explanations include relocation to be nearer to family, continuing education, and childbirth. These reasons prompt discussion that is short, sweet, and all positive. Who would argue with that?

The Job-hopper

Frequency of job movement may raise another concern. *Working professionals who repeatedly leave companies within a year or two after joining are commonly referred to as "job-hoppers."* With the exception of movement across start-ups and tech companies, job-hopping is often looked upon disparagingly by prospective employers. It indicates there has been continual disruption in one's employment history. For many hirers, this is a deal breaker.

Job-hoppers may be viewed as employees who lack focus and direction: they don't know what they want, are easily bored, impatient, or possibly unstable. They may also be regarded as employees who lack loyalty to any company, and who leave before they contribute any value. Job-hoppers are often perceived as people who change jobs only for more money.

Past behavior is a reasonably good predictor of future behavior. So if you job-hop, you are branded as someone who will soon hop again. At the outset of your interview, you will hear the question, *"Why have you moved around so much?"* Be prepared with a positive explanation. You will have to convince a hiring manager that you are a worthwhile investment.

Hiring decisions are critical, and managers expend a lot of resources and energy to get it right. Vacant jobs can take months to fill. Any number of candidates may be interviewed during that time. If a new hire stays for only a year or so (often less), the hiring process has to start all over again. Thus, the chance that a new hire would leave the company after a short tenure is a serious consideration for a hirer.

There is an obvious exception. In today's world of ever-changing technologies and constant shifts from brick and mortar to e-commerce, new companies and industries are popping up, exploding, and transforming so quickly that employees have to change with them in order to survive. In many high-risk, high-reward industries today, there is really no precedent for how long an employee stays in one place.

It's also typical for professionals on the fast track to change jobs frequently to earn a quick promotion and big money. This strategy can be very successful if you are a rock star. But it may prompt the question, "Why didn't your previous employers step up?" A fast-tracker can usually talk her way through frequent movement, but to maintain credibility she had better deliver the goods when she shows up.

A Layoff Is No Longer a Stigma

A generation ago, job security was the norm, and any mention of a layoff was taboo. Employees who were laid off were personally devastated, embarrassed, and unsure how to pick up the pieces and start over. Today all this has changed. Job security is no longer the norm, and a layoff is no longer a stigma. It is simply a sign of our times.

Being laid off is different than being fired. Companies today are in a continual state of reorganization which leads to downsizing and outsourcing. Many employees fall victim to the turmoil and lose their jobs. This practice has become typical across many industries. Now when a candidate has been laid off, some hiring managers don't even ask why. So there is no need to be nervous about discussing it. If you have been laid off and are asked about it on a job interview, just tell your story

CHAPTER 10

What to Do About Timing

Timing is Everything!

We all find ourselves on the job market for different reasons. There are matters of urgency at one extreme and casual exploration at the other. Where you fall on this spectrum determines the importance of timing for you. If you are passively seeing what's out there, timing is less important. You're probably employed or at least not desperate about finding a job. You can be selective about the jobs you pursue, and you have the luxury to pursue one job at a time. However, if you're unemployed or aggressively searching for a job, you may be juggling multiple interviews with several companies at the same time. We wonder *what to do about timing* when the position we really want is still out there while less exciting prospects begin to materialize. In this case, timing is everything!

Manage Your Interview Scheduling

When you are interviewing with more than one company, you must proactively manage your interview scheduling. If you're lucky, your competing interviews will move somewhat in tandem and you'll wrap up all your activity within a one- to two-week window. More likely, you will not be so lucky. Instead, you may need to buy time for the companies that are moving slowly by delaying your interviews with the ones that are moving more quickly.

If you delay interviews, you must have a very good reason for doing so. Project deadlines, mandatory meetings, and business travel sometimes pop up with short notice. Most interviewers understand that. But, if a hiring manager senses you are stalling due to a lack of interest, she may decide not to proceed with you. *Managers expect you to be excited about their job and to prioritize interviewing with them.* Dragging your feet implies you are not serious, or that your greater interest lies elsewhere.

Manage Your Response to a Job Offer

If you get a job offer from the company that is your first choice, timing is irrelevant. Negotiate the offer (if necessary), and accept the job. However, *if you get an offer from a less preferred company first, you must manage your response to the offer very carefully.*

Always be appreciative to any company that has extended a job offer. Start by thanking them, and reiterate your interest in the position. Let them know you are in the late stages of interviewing with another firm, and as a courtesy, you would like to let that firm also complete its process with you before you make a decision. This position is generally respected by the first mover, because had they *not* moved first, they would have appreciated the same courtesy. Of course, *do not* disclose that they are not your first choice. (In fact, your ranking may change!)

The firm will ask when they should expect your response. Inquire if you may get back to them with a status of your timeline within a couple of days. Hopefully by then you'll know when you can respond with a decision.

Now you have to move quickly. Ideally, within the same day of receiving your offer, let your preferred company know you've received an offer from another firm and face a deadline by which you have to respond. Don't be nervous about telling them. If you are their candidate of choice, you are doing them a big favor. They do not want to lose you! Tell them they are your top pick. Let them know you will make yourself available at their convenience to complete the interview process if they are interested. You must balance your communication very carefully. Give the company enough incentive to move along quickly, but not so much pressure that they decide they can't possibly meet your timeframe. You don't want them to back out of the process.

Typically, companies expect a response to their job offer within one week (give or take). If you need more time (as you will when you are waiting on another company), weigh your need to stall against the company's need to fill the job. Be sure it's worth stalling. If the preferred company doesn't come through with an offer (or comes through with an unsatisfactory one), you may ultimately accept the offer in your hands. Or you may want to keep the door open for other possible opportunities in the future. Make sure they continue to feel good about you! Try to respond within two weeks at the most. After that, a company begins to lose interest in you.

You don't have to disclose any information about your competing job offers or interviewing activity to any firm. However, if you are at the offer stage with the firm you want to join, it behooves you to share any information that may help close the deal. For instance, if they ask about an offer you're already holding, it's usually because they want to meet it or beat it. If they tell you they can't, you may want to remind them that they're your first choice, and tell them you are flexible (if you are). You want to get an offer from them! Don't let them walk away.

Your Due Diligence

You owe it to yourself to finish as much interviewing activity as possible and to do your due diligence in evaluating your job offers. A short-sighted decision poses risk. If you accept a job prematurely and it ends up not being right for you, you may renege on your acceptance, resign shortly after starting, or be unhappy at a job you could have weeded out. On the other hand, if you decline an offer before doing your research, you may forgo a great opportunity. Any hiring manager should respect a reasonable time-frame within which you will respond to his offer. If he doesn't, you might want to reconsider whether you want to work for him.

Experienced and savvy job candidates sometimes accept job offers and still continue to interview. This usually happens when they are pressured for a response while their other interviewing activity is still in prog-ress. They want to be sure there isn't a better oppor-tunity out there before they start the new job. If they re-ceive a better offer, they renege on their former ac-ceptance. This strategy is understandable, but it's not optimal for either party. It puts the candidate in the awk-ward position of doing damage control, and it leaves the hiring company to start its talent search all over again.

However, choosing the right job is an important life decision, and it may be a long-term one. You owe it to yourself to make the best possible move. Most often, job offers are not conveniently synchronized. *Use your best judgment to manage timing, and always be respectful and professional in your communication.*

Part III

Take Nothing
for Granted

CHAPTER 11

Having a Successful Interview Does Not Mean Getting the Job

What Defines Success?

A successful job interview is one you leave knowing you have given the best possible presentation of your professional self. You demonstrated your know-ledge, skills, strengths, and even your developmental opportunities. You presented detailed examples of your experience, and while doing so, you displayed your professional style. You offered thoughtful insights about the position, business, and company, and provided sincere and respectable reasons why you want to work there. You asked intelligent and informed questions and created an environment where all parties were enthusiastically engaged. You did your best, and left a lasting positive impression with the team.

However, *having a successful interview does not mean getting the job.* Whether or not you get the job is a different question entirely.

Answer the Unasked Questions

You will always possess some relevant qualifications that you are not asked about during an interview. Some may be invaluable in positioning you as the strongest contender, even if they are not required for the job. Don't let any of your key attributes go unmentioned. *Even if the "right" questions are not asked, make sure you answer them!*

Highlight your additional strengths at the close of the interview when you are asking your final questions. Tell the hiring manager that you have other experience you would like to share because it may be relevant to the hiring decision.

Perhaps you have experience managing staff, but the position doesn't require it. Mention this experience because it highlights your leadership potential. This may prompt the manager to think about your long-term value to the company. Employers look to hire employees they can groom for managerial roles.

Perhaps you are bilingual or trilingual but the job doesn't require it. If the hiring company is a global one, your linguistic skills may increase your growth potential and value to the firm tremendously.

Or maybe you have an innate affinity for the industry in which you are interviewing. For example, you may come from a long line of medical professionals and naturally desire to build your own career in the health-services field. Or perhaps there is someone close to you whose personal health situation is driving you to a career in medical research or to a non-profit cause that will express your passion. If so, say so. An employee who is passionate about his job is likely to work hard, be happy, and stay for the long term.

Today professionals commonly educate themselves on new technologies. If you are self-taught in any relevant areas, disclose it. Hiring managers look for people who are self-motivated and take initiative to learn and grow.

Once you have left all your valuable assets on the table, you have had a successful interview! A less successful interview is one you leave remembering all the wonderful qualities about yourself that you forgot to mention.

You May Never Know Why You Were Declined

One of life's valuable lessons is: do not take anything personally. This is very hard to do when you are talking about rejection after a job interview. There is always some degree of anxiety associated with interviewing, and not getting an offer can be extremely disappointing.

You will probably never know why you were not selected for a specific job. The outcome of the interview process depends on too many factors that are external to you. Try not to overanalyze the outcome, and do not take it personally.

You may be an excellent candidate but you may not be the best match for the team's current needs. The existing talent and dynamics of the hiring organization are a major consideration in the hiring decision. A work group aims to optimize its productivity as a whole, so it looks not only for the skills that are required for the role but also for other useful skills that are underrepresented on the team. The ideal hire is one whose profile best complements the team's current makeup.

Fit is critical for an organization, as well it should be. Teamwork is vital, so an organization cannot afford to be knocked off-kilter by a new hire. Unfortunately, fit is determined exclusively by the interviewing team, and you will never really know what "fit" means for them.

Sometimes a firm's hiring activity suddenly shuts down due to a shift in corporate priorities. This could mean a company reorganization, budget cuts, a hiring freeze, or something else. The job vacancy closes or is put on an indefinite hold, and a hire never happens.

Movement of employees in the work group may also halt hiring activity. A manager or team member may resign or move to another role, causing a change in hiring priorities. Replacing an incumbent usually takes precedence over filling other vacancies.

Realignment of a hiring team while a talent search is in progress may cause a vacant role to be redefined and a different search to begin. The position that is ultimately filled may end up looking nothing like the role that was first advertised. Thus, the profile of the new hire may be different than that which the hiring team had originally set out to find.

Sometimes companies search extensively for external candidates but end up moving an internal resource into the job. An internal employee's career progression usually supersedes the hire of an external resource. So essentially there is no actual hire at all.

A company's hiring activity may also be driven by its clients' needs. If a company loses a major client, hiring typically ceases.

Also, if you are overqualified for a job, you are unlikely to be hired for the position. Despite a candidate's level of interest, hiring managers tend not to hire overqualified candidates because they are usually underutilized and bored. They often leave as soon as they find a level-appropriate job. Similarly, hirers are unlikely to put a sharp, smart, talented go-getter into a mundane, monotonous dead-end job. Consider yourself lucky if you are never mismatched in this way. It's very difficult to stay motivated in a job that doesn't challenge you.

If you know you said or did something during the interview or neglected to say or do something that led to the rejection of your candidacy, work on fixing it for your next opportunity. *But realize there are many things happening behind the scenes that have nothing to do with you.* Value the experience, and move on.

CHAPTER 12

Lunch Is Never Lunch

Remember You Are on a Job Interview!

Most on-site job interviews last a minimum of two hours and sometimes fill the better part of an entire work day. For full-day interviews, lunch with one or more interviewers is usually included on the agenda. On a job interview, *lunch is never lunch*; it is part of the formal interview process.

If the interviewers who have been scheduled to have lunch with you are meeting you for the first time, you are making a first impression. *Conduct yourself exactly as you would at their office.* You want their opinion of you to be reflective of your professionalism and talent, not your eating habits, table manners, and lunchtime humor. These folks have probably been given the lunch shift because they were unable to break away from their desks during regular business hours to interview you. They deserve and expect the same presentation of your qualifications as their colleagues got back at the office. And their feedback on your performance is as important as the feedback from every other interviewer.

Don't Let Your Guard Down

In a casual setting, it is very easy to become too familiar with an interviewer and veer the conversation off course. It's also hard to concentrate, listen, and maintain your composure in a crowded and noisy restaurant or cafeteria. Your performance is not excused for the distractions. Stay sharp and focused. Do not minimize the discussion. Think carefully. Be articulate. Be comprehensive. Expect questions. Ask questions. Do not let your guard down, and remember to keep your humor in check. *Do not cheat yourself out of having a great interview because you are at lunch.*

I recall an instance when a candidate blew an entire interview over lunch. She was a perfect fit for the role based on her qualifications. But during lunch, she initiated random conversation that was inappropriate. This could be talk about anything such as politics, religion, personal problems, or controversial news. Avoid these topics! You are on a formal job interview. You must stay the course, and always conduct yourself professionally.

It's Time to Eat

Eat something light before you head out to interview. You don't want to feel sluggish while interviewing, but you don't want your stomach to rumble either. You need to stay focused on the interview, not on the upcoming meal.

For lunch, make your food selection wisely so you stay alert and clean. Eat quietly while the interviewer is doing the talking, and eat sparingly so your mouth is not full when you are asked a question. Refrain from alcoholic beverages, even if a team member invites you to join him. You are on a formal interview. Your job is to stay lucid and steady, so politely decline. If you are invited to happy hour after the interview, use your best judgment of the situation when ordering your beverage. You don't want to have any regrets when the interview day is behind you.

CHAPTER 13

It's More Than Just a Thank-You Note

To Write or Not to Write...That is the Question

Do you think a job candidate receives a job offer because he sent a thank-you note to the hiring manager or interviewer? Likely not. A person receives a job offer because he is the best fit for a position at the time of hire, not because he wrote a note.

Do you think a lead candidate might be declined an offer because he *did not* write a note? Probably not. If a hiring team is ready to move forward with its first choice, the lack of a forthcoming note is unlikely to change that. In fact, the hire may precede the receipt of any note if the hiring team is quick to move.

Lastly, do you believe a lead candidate might be declined an offer because he did write a note? Absolutely—if the note diminishes his candidacy.

I remember when a lead candidate wrote a note—a poorly written one—and the hiring manager decided to stop the final offer process before the job offer was extended. The person's writing skills were unacceptable to him. This is a devastating outcome for any candidate, especially when strong writing skills are not even required for the job!

One More Test to Pass

A thank-you note is more than just a thank-you note. It's an example of your written communication skills. By sending a note, you are giving yourself one more interview test to pass— and you must pass the test!

If you write a thank-you note, it must impress the reader. Your note must be *excellent*—in appearance, content, tone, and timing. It should contain a few sentences within one or two short paragraphs conveying why you are interested in the role and how you will contribute to the business. Simply saying "thank you" to remind an interviewer that you are still out there does not help your candidacy.

The tone of your note must be professional, never informal. Your voice should reflect humility rather than boastfulness, and your enthusiasm must never be misconstrued as desperation. You should be perceived as interested, qualified, and impressive. Your grammar must be excellent, and your presentation neat, whether it's handwritten or typed. Have an appropriate reader proofread it.

Don't pounce on a hiring manager or interviewer with a note immediately following your interview. Give yourself a day to digest what you've learned, and collect your thoughts before you write. You want the hirer to know you have seriously considered the opportunity and are genuinely interested. Then send out your note within a day or two at the most. After that, a busy manager has forgotten you.

If you are a fresh graduate or junior applicant with little or no work experience, you may want to send a thank-you note. You are in a pool of mostly indiscernible talent, so your note helps to position you as a courteous and engaged candidate. As your career progresses, your qualifications become increasingly unique and distinguishable. In a pool of experienced and diverse talent, a lead candidate ultimately emerges, and a thank-you note becomes less relevant.

Always Say "Thank You"

Always thank each interviewer for taking the time to interview you. Ask the hiring manager about next steps in the process, and let him know you look forward to hearing back.

You will thank your interviewers over the phone and again in person. If you feel the need to thank them yet again in writing, be sure your writing skills are up to the challenge. *If you have any doubt, play it safe. Take a pass on the thank-you note.*

CHAPTER 14

Select the Right References

Who Are Your References?

When a job candidate is near the end of a job interview process, the hiring company typically asks her to provide professional (and sometimes personal) references. At this point, she is usually close to receiving a job offer, but the deal is not sealed just yet. The hiring manager looks for solid, even bulletproof references to move the candidate forward. This is a critical step in the interview process. *One bad reference can end the process immediately.*

Protocol for securing references is to respectfully ask a person to act as a reference for you, not to assume he will do so without your asking. *Be thoughtful and strategic in making your selections.* Your references should be professionals who know you well. They should be ones who can give a convincing account of your professional qualifications as well as your personal attributes.

Most job seekers know not to choose someone who doesn't like them or someone with whom they've encountered any sort of conflict in the past. Rather they select former managers, advisors, professors, peers, or clients who thought most highly of their work and would desire to work with them again. However, never assume you know what someone is going to say about you. Nor should you expect him to know what to say until he understands the role for which you are interviewing. *You must manage the success of your own reference checks.* It is devastating to get all the way through the interview process only to have the whole thing fall apart with your references.

Your Selection Criteria

Your references must be excellent and secure your job offer. Ask each reference upfront if he is able to give you an

A+ (excellent) reference. Ask each to be honest with you. A person is doing you a great disservice if he agrees to provide a reference and then provides a less than enthusiastic one, or worse, a bad one. If he agrees to provide a B reference (good), and tells you so in advance, you can continue to look for another A+ before you settle for his B. However, you won't be able to control all of your "grades." Most companies require at least one reference from a former manager, so you will be stuck with that grade—good or bad.

Ensuring outstanding grades from your references is not where your selection criteria should stop. *You should select people with solid communication skills who can express themselves intelligibly and advocate for you.* The credibility and strength of your references will depend on the sincerity and conviction with which they are presented. A lackluster or sloppy delivery of an otherwise strong reference may be misconstrued as weak and give the decision-maker undue pause. Never let a reference's communication skills put your job offer in jeopardy.

Coach Your References!

Don't ever let a reference get a cold call from a company that is interviewing you. He'll be caught off guard and will have to collect his thoughts about you on the spot. The spontaneity may hurt you.

Instead, coach your references so they are alert and well prepared to secure your job offer! Tell each reference about the company and the job for which you are interviewing. Highlight your work experience, skills, and personal attributes that are most relevant for the role. Be sure everyone covers your key strengths and attributes so they substantiate each others' claims. Give them *different* points to address with respect to your unique work relationship as well. Their referrals should not be redundant but rather provide a comprehensive view of your talent. Provide examples that support your candidacy since the details have probably been forgotten since you worked together.

Regarding your work experience and skills, your references should identify your areas of expertise. They should discuss your credentials, knowledge, aptitude, and achievement. Remind them of work projects you completed and other challenges you tackled successfully while

115

you worked together. You might ask them to discuss your work efficiency and effectiveness, for example, your ability to think clearly and quickly, assess business needs astutely, gather information, multitask, problem-solve, and streamline execution. If the role requires management of staff, ask them to address your leadership experience. One might discuss your success mentoring and empowering others. Another might discuss your experience resolving conflict and give examples of human resource issues you successfully managed.

Coach your references to discuss your personal attributes as well. *A prospective employer is interested not only in your experience and skills necessary to do the job, but also in your potential to do the job successfully.* She wants to assess your personality, work ethic, and overall fit for the position, team, and organization. She wants to know your desire for learning, your degree of curiosity and creativity, your talent for thinking critically and strategically, and your ability to use sound judgment. She tries to gauge your tolerance for stressful work situations and demanding clients, and your flexibility or resistance to change.

With regard to your personal attributes, a reference might mention that you are always punctual and never miss meetings or deadlines. He might discuss the strong positive feedback from your customers and their formal recognition of your excellent support. One might discuss how you are sought out by other departments as a go-to person because of both your expertise and your willingness to help coworkers. Or perhaps you've been shuffled across several internal roles within a short time and have proven unflappable with every move.

Hirers conduct reference checks to reinforce their decision to hire you. They look and listen for convincing reasons to move forward with a job offer while observing any red flags in the process. You must s*elect the right references*, and coach them properly!

Part IV

Let's Talk Money

CHAPTER 15

Your Salary Requirement

How the Talk Goes

In a growing number of states today, employers are banned from asking job candidates about their salary history. However, expect to be asked for *your salary requirement*. This can be awkward for any candidate. Many have no idea what to say. Some are afraid to bid themselves too high; others are afraid to sell themselves short. And many candidates are just not sure what their skills are worth on the job market.

Let the hirer initiate any discussion regarding salary. A job seeker who is first to mention money often gives the impression that the salary is more important than the role. This may be true, but greedy people are risky hires; they usually leave a job as soon as they find another that pays more. If an employer thinks you are focused only on the money, he will probably pass.

You may be asked for your salary requirement at any time. If you're asked before the interview process begins, it's usually because the hiring company wants to make sure they can afford you before proceeding. No one wants to waste anyone's time. Typically, the talk happens at the end of the interview process after both parties have vetted the job to be done and the skills required to do it.

What Is My Salary Requirement?

Stating your salary requirement can be tricky because you want to sound informed and not say the "wrong" number. If you're not pushed for a hard number, targeting fair market value is a respectable way to go. *You may want to position your salary requirement within a range.* This lets the hirer know you are flexible, and this gives her some leeway.

There are several common ways to determine a reasonable salary requirement. First, know whether the salary range for the position has been disclosed. If the hiring manager asks if you know it, she may be fishing to see if you've done your homework. This range is ideal for setting your target. Staying within range is the safest bet if you really want the job. If you request a salary above the maximum, be prepared to explain why. If you have to relocate to take the job, for example, you might request more money to make the move economically feasible. Just be aware that if you're not flexible, your candidacy may be dismissed if your requirement exceeds their budget.

Second, consider your current salary (or most recent salary if you are unemployed) a baseline for setting your requirement. Typically, a professional on a steady and progressive career path realizes an increase to their base salary of roughly ten to twenty percent when they change jobs (depending on job level). Any number in that range is a reasonable request. Or if your current salary is comfortable for you, you may be fine asking for the same amount. In fact, if you changed jobs within the past year (or if you job-hop), you may already be at fair market value (or higher) for your level of experience. Be careful not to overshoot a sensible salary for the job you really want. You may price yourself out of consideration.

Third, you may want to explore the use of online salary calculators. Today they are popular for identifying and comparing market salaries across jobs, companies, industries, and geographies. These tools can be very helpful when used with good judgment, but there are limitations. For example, most job titles are generic. This can be problematic because job title is a key input to the tool. The job function (depth and breadth of the role and responsibilities) really has to be captured in an analysis in order to make any meaningful comparisons. And for some up-and-coming companies today, job titles are already obsolete or quickly fading away.

Another limitation is that output depends on input. The data that a user inputs to an online salary calculator depends on his interpretation of the particular information the tool is looking for. In some cases, the input is accurate. In other cases, it's a guess. In all cases, it's subject to human error, and we all make mistakes. So a user should be aware that the reliability of any answer depends on the validity of the input data of the users—those who report information to the tool and those who request information from it. It's always best to position your findings within a sensible range to offset any error.

Finally, talk with people. Reach out to your trusted colleagues, peers, or friends in comparable positions to let them know you are on the job market. Explain the role for which you are interviewing, and ask if they have a sense of the salary you should target. Some may be open to sharing their compensation with you or giving you a fair range you can work with.

We all want to earn the salary we feel our talent is worth. But our research is key to knowing how to fairly position ourselves relative to the market. *Use as much information as possible to set a range for your requirement.* You should be confident when you state the pay you require for the job.

Quoting a Firm Number

If you have a firm salary requirement and will not work for a penny less, be sure you are committed to the number and ready to walk away before you put it on the table. You risk ending your candidacy abruptly if the firm cannot afford you. Be sure you're okay with this outcome. The hirer may ask if you have wiggle room, but if you've already stated that your requirement is firm, she probably won't bother. Don't play games. If you suddenly have flexibility, it means your requirement wasn't really firm to begin with.

A hiring manager is looking to hire someone who wants the job she is offering, not just any job at some targeted salary. If you are too focused on the money, she may be turned off. And if she perceives you are an inflexible person in general, she may choose to pass rather than find out you are difficult to work with.

Stating a firm salary requirement can also corner you. If you receive a higher offer from another company, you may want to revisit the hard number you already put on the table. This is off-putting to a firm that has already agreed to meet it. You don't want to undersell yourself, but you have to consider whether doing the necessary damage control is worth it.

CHAPTER 16

There Are Many Reasons to Take a Pay Cut

There is More to Life than Money

We all look forward to an increase in pay when we change jobs. But when non-monetary factors make a career opportunity very attractive, we are often willing to compromise on salary. There are trade-offs. Only you can decide which trade-offs are worth it.

Career advancement is one of the most common reasons for job movement. This may mean more money now, or more money later. More money later sometimes translates to less money now, but on a more promising career path. The trade-off of money for opportunity is often an excellent long-term career strategy.

Better work-life balance is another common reason why people are willing to compromise on salary when changing jobs. The trade-off is money for personal time. This could mean flexible work hours, a shorter commute, work-at-home arrangements, elimination of excessive travel, or something else. In fact, if your current job requires heavy travel, you are probably paid handsomely for it. You are compensated for the inconvenience as well as for the time added to your work schedule. When you change jobs for one that minimizes or eliminates travel, you should *expect* less pay. If there is a spouse, small children, or elderly parents at home, a job without travel or one that offers flextime or remote reporting is priceless.

Trading off money for happiness is arguably the easiest compromise to make. If you are relocating to be closer to your family or friends, you may willingly trade off salary even in a higher cost of living area. Elimination of an undesirable work situation such as a bad boss, constant burn-out, or extreme boredom, is perhaps the most liberating reason to accept less pay. Accommodating the personal circumstances of your spouse or partner, children, or parents can make life happier for everyone.

Certainly, when you make a job change, the economics have to make sense for you. But many people who look beyond money often come out the richer for it.

Benefits and Perks

A job offer is an entire package, of which salary is only one component. Employee benefits are a significant part of the package. Some job candidates readily take a pay cut for better benefits. In fact, some job changes are driven exclusively by a need or desire to secure benefits. *Don't evaluate a salary offer independent of the benefits!*

An employee benefits package generally includes health insurance, disability coverage, retirement savings plans, paid holidays, and vacation time. Tuition reimbursement is also common. Relocation assistance may be a large part of your benefits package if you have to relocate to take the job. Each package has its own variation, so be sure to study the details carefully. Know exactly what is included in your benefits when evaluating your job offer.

Health benefits can represent thousands to tens of thousands of dollars per year in an employee's compensation package depending on whether he is insuring himself alone or other family members as well. Long-term savings and/or pension plans and stock can add any number of dollars to one's long-term income based mostly on job level and tenure.

Tuition reimbursement is a valuable benefit that many employers offer to grow their human capital investment—*you!* And their investment pays *you* huge dividends. Your education not only improves your ability to do your present job, it also enhances your credentials and marketability over the long run. Consider exhausting your tuition reimbursement benefit whether you had originally planned on it or not.

Additional benefits or perks include on-site health and fitness centers, on-site child care facilities, or cash discounts for these or other types of products and services. Casual-dress environments, early-dismissal Fridays, free food, and on-site sports facilities have become quite popular in recent years. And, let's not forget Fido. Pet health insurance has added a warm touch to the benefits package for many pet owners. These benefits and perks don't usually make or break one's decision to accept a job offer, but they do help to sweeten the deal.

Manage Your Ego

Don't let your ego (we all have one) cloud your judgment when evaluating a job offer you want to accept. *Regardless of how talented you are, a company's budget may not meet your salary expectations.* There may be no reason to turn down a great opportunity if the compensation package is workable for you. The happier you are in your job, the more productive you'll likely be. Your merit increases and advancement opportunities should reflect that. Over time, the salary you earned walking in the door becomes less relevant.

There are many reasons to take a pay cut. Think about this seriously before turning down the job you want because of less pay.

CHAPTER 17

Negotiate Professionally

Do I Want This Job?

Many job candidates think that when they receive a job offer, the hiring company expects them to negotiate. This may be true. *But there is one question you should ask yourself before you begin any salary negotiation: "Do I want this job?"*

Negotiate professionally. Only negotiate a job offer you are considering accepting. Once a company decides to make you an offer, it could take days, weeks, or longer to get the formal offer to you. The legwork required to complete the administrative process takes time. When a company's job offer is negotiated, this process begins all over again. Be respectful of the process.

Don't negotiate a job offer you intend to decline. To ask a company for more money, have them repeat the entire approval process and deliver a better number, then turn them down is not a professional way to negotiate. It wastes their time. Some candidates do this to bid up their price so they can leverage it with other companies. This may seem like a wise strategy, but you might burn a bridge with a company you want to work for in the future. This doesn't mean you have to accept any job offer you negotiate. You may intend to accept an offer but ultimately decline if the outcome of the negotiation is unacceptable to you. Just leave negotiation for jobs you want, not for jobs you don't want.

Begin a negotiation by thanking the hiring contact for the offer. (The hiring contact may be the hiring manager or an HR partner.) Tell her you are excited about the opportunity and plan to join, so you would like to discuss the details of the offer package. *Companies do their best for people who are serious and enthusiastic, and who put their commitment to join on the table.*

Don't be afraid to negotiate. When you receive a job offer, it means that the company wants you to join. They would much rather negotiate with you than see you walk away. The manager looks forward to hearing "Yes!" not "No thanks." If they lose you, they have to go with their second choice or begin the search process all over again.

A Game of Ping-pong

An efficient negotiation is like a game of ping-pong where you hit the ball back only once. A company serves you an offer, and you return with the salary number and parameters you will accept. This strategy eliminates the useless exercise of asking if there is any flexibility, waiting for a response, then finding that the revised offer still does not meet your requirements. One direct return puts your confirmation to accept the offer on the table.

Do your homework before responding to any job offer. *Your salary requirement must be defendable, based on sound economic and logical reasoning, and you must be forthcoming in explaining it.* A carefully calculated response tells the company you have diligently evaluated their offer. You are serious and ready to join. This is a professional negotiation. You are giving the hiring company great incentive to meet your needs. They know the deal is done if they do.

The company may then respond with an improved offer but not match your request. They may also respond with their original offer. At this point, you choose to accept, decline, or initiate a second round of ping-pong. Be aware that a second round puts additional pressure on the company and may be risky. The message you are sending is that you don't really believe they did their best with either their first or second offer. You may be perceived as greedy, arrogant, or more interested in the money than the role. Of course, you may have an excellent defense for round two, and if you do, you must present it professionally. *A hiring company always has the prerogative to continue to negotiate with you or not.* They may stay the course, state their final position, or pull the offer off the table entirely.

Other Levers for Negotiation

Salary is not the only part of a job offer that you can negotiate. Much of the benefits package is negotiable, and there are many ways to negotiate it. Sign-on bonuses, relocation assistance, stock options, and vacation days are some of the most common items that candidates negotiate. Some benefits are non-negotiable due to corporate policies, but you will never know unless you ask.

You might request that your health benefits start on the first day of employment rather than after some designated waiting period. You might ask that your initial performance review and subsequent merit increase occur sooner than the year-end standard. Perhaps you need miscellaneous funds to break a lease or to move household goods if no relocation package is offered; you may ask for help with these expenses. Non-salary items are often negotiated when the salary itself is non-negotiable. This helps to sweeten the pot when the salary is firm.

Work-at-home arrangements and flexible work hours are popular items for negotiation. With all requests, manage your expectations reasonably. You may know you are a star performer who is self-motivated and effective at working remotely, no matter what the role. However, it may be unrealistic to expect you'll do so upon hire when no one really knows you. Your manager will want to observe your performance in the office before you become invisible to him. He'll want to know you have a good handle on the job and are building strong relationships with your coworkers and clients. And you'll have to demonstrate that your work ethic suggests a productive work-at-home arrangement. A realistic expectation may be that you would work on site for the first three to six months of employment. This is a small inconvenience to enable your optimal work situation.

Don't Let Your Job Offer Be Rescinded

A hiring company may stop the hiring process with you at any time. Having a job offer withdrawn can be devastating. There are many reasons why job offers are rescinded.

Always be respectful with your response to any job offer. A person who goes missing after receiving an offer is regarded as unprofessional and rude. If you're not sure about your decision, or are waiting for other competing offers to come in, communicate to the hiring contact that you need additional time to consider the offer before responding. If your timeframe is reasonable (say, a week), a company is likely to agree without hesitation. If you drag the process out longer with half-hearted or no communication, he may decide to rescind the offer rather than wait any longer.

An offer may be rescinded when a candidate requests an exorbitant salary or unreasonable increase to any part of the offer package. If you and the employer are too far apart on the numbers, the company may pull back the offer because you are being unrealistic or because they are simply unable to meet it. Employers do not hire people they cannot make happy. If you aren't happy with a company's offer from the outset, you may not be happy with its annual merit increases and bonus payouts either. No employer invests in an unsatisfied new hire. He will leave as soon as a better offer comes along.

An offer may also fall through when a job requires relocation or reflects a change of industry and the candidate's estimation of his fair market value in the respective markets does not align with that of the hiring company. I remember an incident when a candidate and hiring contact used online salary calculators to conduct a negotiation for a job which required relocation. They compared the candidate's current salary and proposed salary in the respective locations, and reached opposite conclusions! The candidate calculated that his compensation should be higher in the new location while the hiring contact calculated that it should be lower. There was much debate, but no resolution. Though the offer was not officially rescinded, both parties ultimately agreed to disagree and walk away.

In fact, a candidate can easily price himself out of a job if his salary requirement exceeds fair market value for the respective market. Use your best judgment, and weigh your need for money against your desire for the job. For the most part, a company's internal compensation policy determines who the company can afford. Even if you are a superior candidate and the manager wants to hire you, he may be tightly bound by the rules.

However, if the new job is a promotion or carries greater financial risk, for instance, your request for more money may be substantiated and fulfilled. Regardless of your reason for requesting a higher salary, you must explain and defend your position. You don't ever want a company to be turned off by you. This could take your offer off the table.

You may also have your job offer rescinded if you exhibit any unpleasant behavior before the process ends. Some interviewees become impatient by the length of the formal hiring process. Keep your emotions in check. Securing the verbal offer, moving from verbal to written offer, and completing the necessary background checks can take several weeks and sometimes longer. If you are intolerant of the process, you could be dismissed as someone who is arrogant, inflexible, and probably difficult to work with.

I recall a tremendous interviewing debacle with a superior senior-level candidate. This gentleman was so exceptional that the hiring team started putting together an offer for him while he was still interviewing. They loved him, and the offer was almost out on the spot. While the man was waiting for the final interviewer, his attitude changed. He became noticeably irritated, feeling disrespected because his time was being wasted. The firm's offer consideration ended immediately. Regardless of his outstanding credentials, no one wanted to work with him.

Never negotiate a job offer you do not have. Unless a company has extended a formal job offer, do not discuss your concerns or expectations regarding compensation, benefits, relocation, etc. (unless you are specifically asked to do so). Be patient and let the process unfold naturally. Once an offer is made, you'll have all the information you need about the total package, and you can then decide whether negotiation is necessary. Candidates who start voicing concerns and putting demands on the table before a company has decided to hire them are perceived as presumptuous, overly confident, and too aggressive.

Don't give any potential employer any reason to doubt she can work with you. Stay on your toes until the bitter end, and take nothing for granted. The hiring process isn't over until it's over!

CHAPTER 18

Resign Your Job and Your Guilt

Get Hired First!

*I*f you are resigning your job to move to a new one, confirm that you are officially hired before you resign. A company's hiring activity can stop in an instant. Corporate priorities shift, policies change, and people move. Your hire may be delayed, put on hold indefinitely, or the worst case—declined. You *never* want to be in a position where you have resigned your job, and the new one falls through.

Contact your new employer to get a final confirmation that you are officially hired. Ask if all required paperwork is in place and complete with authorized signatures. Inquire if all background checks are finalized, and if the results of any required drug tests are acceptable. Then set a start date. Once the hiring party has confirmed your official hire, you are good to go!

Some of Us Look Back

Some people can boldly resign, bid their manager good riddance, and never look back. But many of us have a very hard time resigning from a job. It can be extremely unsettling to tell your boss you are leaving, especially if the workload is great, and you know he'll be surprised. If he has treated you well, it's natural to feel guilty and responsible for disappointing him. However, *your decision to resign is a personal career decision. There is no reason to feel guilty about it.*

Regardless of your reason for leaving, always keep the discussion positive, respectful, and professional. You want to maintain a mutually beneficial relationship with your former manager, and keep the door open. You will probably need his help or reference going forward, and you may even find yourself working with him again in the future.

When broaching the subject, referencing the well-being of your family as the reason for leaving is the easiest way to go. If your resignation is due in part to any family circumstances, disclose it. The point is that you *have* to leave, so there is no reason to belabor the discussion. Mention of career advancement or more money leads to a lengthier conversation if your boss wants to retain you. She will likely want to defend how she can help grow your career within the company before she accepts your resignation. She may also raise the opportunity of a pay increase.

The Counteroffer

A company's most common retention play is to put more money on the table. If you are a valued employee and your role is critical to the business, your manager may extend a counteroffer and ask you to stay.

A counteroffer can give you pause, even when your decision was firm coming into the discussion. And it can make you feel unappreciative to turn down a manager who is making a plea to retain you. However, don't let emotion cloud your judgment. With all due respect to you, a counteroffer is often motivated by a manager's need to solve his immediate problem of having to backfill your job. It's rarely because the company cannot survive without you.

If a higher salary is your primary goal and the counteroffer lets you achieve it, your decision may be a simple one. But don't let the lure of money undermine the success of your job market effort without serious consideration of the consequences of staying put any longer. First, remember your career goals. Continued employment with the same company and industry may or may not align with your long-term plans. Also, realize that the familiarity and stability of your current work environment will not remain unchanged forever. Companies merge, spin off, implode, go belly-up, or otherwise go out of business. Organizations roll out changes in leadership and design, and people move on. Suddenly, your work environment is not so familiar or stable anymore.

Be true to yourself, and trust your instincts. If the counteroffer feels like the better decision for you, then seriously consider accepting it. Better compensation together with your established reputation and tenure may make you rethink a move. *But remember why you are on the job market in the first place.* If you seek career growth and are driven to embrace a new and exciting change, move on. Don't let a manager's needs or interests be the reason you stay at a job. This is *your* career. If the time is right, **resign your job and your guilt.** Celebrate your well-deserved job market success, and move on confidently to your next great career opportunity!

CONCLUSION

Thank you for reading *Your Best Job Interview*. It has been a passion project, and I'm excited to share it with you. I want to impress on you two key points of the book.

First, shift your focus from hard to soft skills. Certain hard skills are required for every job. We study hard, acquire skills, and go after jobs that best match our talent. But soft skills are often more important. You are observed by every interviewer you meet during the interview process, from start to finish. You are observed by your boss, peers, staff, clients, and superiors every day of your career. Impressions are firm and unforgettable. This is ultimately what determines your success.

Second, be confident, respectful, and always professional. You are ready for your best job interview! Do you remember the young woman I coached for her interview with a top MBA program? I'm sure I hit on most of what I've covered in this book when she and I met. She concluded, "Before we talked, I thought I was going to get into the program. Now, I know I'm getting in!" And she did.

My goal for this book is to leave you more knowledge-able, energized, motivated, and ready to take on your next interview—and the ones that follow. Use it as a resource to remind you of many not-so-obvious aspects of the inter-view process that are so important for your success. And keep interviewing until you find the job you want!

To those of you I know, and to those of you I will meet along my journey, thank you for all I have learned from you and will continue to learn from you in the future. I wish you every success in your career.

—Donna A. Bacon

DONNA A. BACON, Ph.D. has advised and coached employees and job candidates for nearly twenty years. She was an analytics manager for a telecom industry leader for almost a decade, then transitioned to executive recruiting in the analytics field, where she worked with job candidates at all levels of experience across many industries. Throughout her career, Donna supervised teams; recruited, interviewed, and hired staff; and coached many employees through career development. She earned her bachelor's degree in economics from La Salle University and her master's degree and doctorate in economics from the University of Notre Dame.